# HOW TO INTERPRET THE BIBLE

# How to INTERPRET theBIBLE

## ROBERT L. CATE

**BROADMAN PRESS**
Nashville, Tennessee

4211-42
ISBN: 0-8054-1242-9

Dewey Decimal Classification: 220.07
Subject heading: BIBLE—STUDY
Library of Congress Catalog Card Number: 81-86638
*Printed in the United States of America*

DEDICATED TO Ruth
Bob, Jr.
Fred

# Foreword

During my years as a pastor, there were many things which I learned. One of the more important of these was that the real backbone of a church's ministry was that group of dedicated men and women who gave of themselves in teaching the Bible. The roll call of these unsung saints of God is too long to be recounted here. They grappled with the needs of their classes, with the teachings of the Bible, and with a world where it seemed that everything which had been nailed down was coming loose.

We spent much time together, those teachers and I, for we shared the same concerns with trying to make the Bible relevant to life as it is for people as they are. As we grappled with this issue, the single, most common request I received from them was for help in teaching them how to interpret the Scriptures. When I was called away from the pastorate to become a seminary professor, a trainer of those whom God has called to minister, I discovered that these also were seeking for help in interpreting the Scriptures.

Out of those two needs has come this book. It is not a profound treatise on hermeneutics (the science of interpreting the Bible). I will leave that to the technical scholars. Nor is it a simplistic, mechanical approach to the Bible as if it were merely a library of ancient religious literature. I have tried to strike a happy medium between these two extremes. It is a handbook, a guidebook for those who are seeking for a method of biblical interpretation which can be undergirded by prayer and devotion and which can be expected to produce the desired results.

The procedures set forth in this book may at times seem

complicated and complex. Take my word for it, they are not, provided that you deal with them one step at a time.

The task of interpreting the Bible is not easy. It is worth every effort to become a good interpreter of God's revelation for sinful humanity. God loved us enough to give his Son for us. He gave us his written revelation of that love in the Bible. We must love his people enough to learn how to interpret his message to them.

It is my prayer that you will become a good steward of his revelation and of your gifts of interpretation, and that this book will help you to that end.

ROBERT L. CATE
Golden Gate Baptist Theological Seminary
Mill Valley, California

# Contents

## Part 4: Moving from Preparation to Interpretation

## Part 5: Moving from Interpretation to Presentation

# Preface

A chill wind made the huddled figure draw his coat more tightly about him. This helped protect him from the wind but did nothing to ward off the chill that gripped his heart and mind. He was a stranger in a foreign country. Lost and alone, he did not know where his hotel was and could not ask directions from those who passed him by, for he did not speak their language. His only hope had been a map furnished by his hotel, but it too was written in that unknown language. He had never felt so confused, so frightened, or so hopeless.

If you have any imagination at all, you can identify with the plight of our unknown stranger. To be confused, lost, alone, and unable to find help in a strange land must be quite terrifying. With a map which could serve as a guide, the frustration of being unable to understand it has to be completely devastating. Yet this situation, while hypothetical, is also descriptive of the experience of multitudes in their spiritual pilgrimage. Seeking help, they turn to the Bible, but find it difficult (or impossible) to understand. Its language is foreign to them. They need help in understanding God's guide for their lives. They need an interpreter.

It is our task—those of us who bear the responsibility of teaching and preaching God's Word—to guide them. But we must be sure that we are guiding them aright. An interpreter who misunderstands the map is of little help.

## The Need for Good Biblical Interpretation

My simple illustration points up the fact that it is extremely important for anyone who is an interpreter of God's Word to know

**13**

what he or she is doing. Every week millions of people are involved in some form of Bible study, hearing or giving some kind of biblical interpretation. In Sunday Schools, in worship services, in organized and unorganized Bible studies, God's Word is interpreted.

It is bad enough to think of how much time might be wasted by poorly guided Bible studies. It is worse if you believe that the Bible is God's redemptive word to mankind, carrying the directions to life and death. If this is true, then bad biblical interpretation may be death-dealing. Furthermore, if this is true—and it is—our poorly done job of interpreting the Bible may be the stumbling block over which someone falls who is seeking the way of life. The task of interpreting God's Word is an awesome one. It carries tremendous responsibility. It also carries exciting opportunities. What a privilege it is to be able to help people find their way with God by guiding them in understanding his written revelation.

The need for good biblical interpretation is as great as any other human need. If the Bible is what Christians claim it is, God's word to sinful humanity, then it must be taken seriously. We who are responsible for its interpretation must give the task our very best. Anything less is not good enough. We can rejoice in the fact that God can succeed in spite of our failures. But that is no excuse for failing. When we do a good job of interpreting his Word, his Holy Spirit has that much more to work with in speaking to our hearers.

## The Task of Biblical Interpretation

It has been frequently acknowledged by serious students of the Bible that its interpretation is both an art and a science. A little thought will demonstrate the truth of this statement. There is definitely a science to the interpretation of the Bible, in both the Old and the New Testaments. Much poor interpretation fails precisely at this point, when the interpreter neither recognizes nor practices the science of interpretation. A good interpreter must apply the basic techniques of interpretation in their proper order if he (or she) is going to arrive at a correct interpretation of a particular passage. When we neglect the scientific approach to interpretation, we may stumble across the proper interpretation of a passage by accident. It is far more likely, however, that we shall merely stumble in our interpretation. In such a case, we will wind up looking foolish to our audience. That would be bad enough by itself, but it is far worse when we wind up making the Bible look foolish. For that, we shall be held accountable to God. Yet there is hope. Techniques can be learned. Anyone can master a scientific approach to the interpretation of the Bible.

On the other hand, interpreting the Bible is an art. All of the scientific techniques in the world will not necessarily guarantee that an interpreter will produce an understandable, applicable, and correct interpretation. Only by understanding something of the heart of God, the needs of our hearers, and the mind and the spirit of the particular biblical author can we arrive at both a proper and an adequate interpretation. Two painters may have the same technical skills, the same quality of materials, and the same scene to portray. Yet, only one of them produces a work of art. The difference lies neither in technique nor in materials, but in the inner being of the artist. The same is true of the biblical interpreter. Without the proper inner relationship to God, our interpretations will always be inadequate. The inner being of the interpreter certainly determines the quality of the interpretation. This focuses upon the art side of interpretation.

However, we who are called to interpret God's Word must clearly understand that the fact that interpretation is an art based upon our inner relationship with God cannot be used as an excuse for poor technique. *Being rightly related to God is no excuse for shoddy workmanship.* Rather, the reverse is true. As a principle of our stewardship, being rightly related to God demands the very best discipline from those of us called to this ministry of interpreting God's Word to God's people.

We must clearly understand that there are at least two ways in which you and I approach the Bible when we read it. The first of these is for our own personal devotion. The purpose of devotional reading of the Scriptures is to allow God's Holy Spirit to speak through his Word directly to the reader. While such reading of the Scriptures should be done with all of the knowledge of the background and context possible, excessive attention to the techniques of biblical interpretation can interfere with our openness to God's personal word to us. For this kind of Bible reading, we need to avoid getting bogged down in such detail that we do not hear the voice of God. God does speak through his Word in spite of our ignorance or limitations. However, this does not mean that we can ever be content with either ignorance or limitations. Yet, we can hear God speak in spite of these.

The second way in which you and I approach the Scripture is when we are studying it in preparation for interpreting God's revelation to someone else. It is in this connection that the disciplined study which this book describes comes into play. There is a difference between hearing God speak to you and preparing yourself to allow God to speak through you. We as interpreters of God's Word to others must never allow this difference to become confused in our own lives and ministries.

## The Problem in Biblical Interpretation

The basic problem in interpreting the Bible is that too many of us have relied upon the art side of interpretation to the neglect of the scientific side. This has produced a vicious circle of which both we and our audience have become the victims.

This vicious circle begins in ignorance. We just do not know enough about the Bible, its world, its literary background, or the times from which it came. Our ignorance may be only partial, but limited ignorance is still ignorance. When we try to interpret from a position of ignorance, our interpretation cannot help but be built upon a shaky foundation. Teaching or preaching from ignorance either adds our ignorance to the ignorance of our hearers, or insults both them and God by proclaiming as true that which they know to be false. Furthermore, ignorance accepted as fact by us or others gives an even shakier foundation for further interpretation. Thus, we wind up even more ignorant, if that is possible, than when we began. This vicious circle seems merely to compound our ignorance, steadily leading us farther and farther away from the truth. We must not ignore Paul's often repeated statement that he did not want his hearers ignorant (see Rom. 1:13; 11:25; 1 Cor. 10:1; 12:1; 2 Cor. 1:8; 1 Thess. 4:13).

## A Strategy for Developing Skills in Interpretation

The only way we can avoid or escape from this vicious circle is by developing a technique which, if followed, will consistently lead us to an adequate interpretation of any passage in the Bible. Such a technique may be similar but not identical to the procedure for interpreting a passage in any ancient book. The Bible surely belongs in the category of an ancient book, but it is a different kind of book. Therefore, before we seek to develop our technique of interpretation, we must fully understand the nature of the Bible.

If our technique of interpretation is to be valid and effective, it must be designed to fit the nature of the material with which we are dealing. There is no other way. A surgeon and a coroner may use similar techniques in cutting open a human body. But there is a decided difference in the ways by which they apply these techniques, since the surgeon is operating upon a living patient while the coroner is cutting upon a dead body. In the same way, our techniques of interpretation will be similar to those applied to other ancient literary works. But there must be a difference between those techniques and ours which takes into account the differences in the nature of the material which is being interpreted. Therefore, before we can actually begin to design our techniques for interpreting the Bible, we must first carefully identify the fundamental characteristics of the literature of the Bible. Without this preliminary step, our techniques of interpretation will most surely be inadequate. Without this preliminary step, our strategy for developing or improving our skills in interpreting the Bible will be doomed to failure.

# Part 1
## Approaching the Bible to Interpret It

# 1

# The Divine Nature of the Bible

In order to develop an adequate procedure for interpreting the Bible, we must first consider the basic characteristics of this book. It is a unique book, and any method of interpretation must come to grips with its unique characteristics. That which makes it unique is its divine nature. It comes from God. At the same time, the Bible also has much in common with many ancient books. These common characteristics reflect its human nature and must also be given serious consideration by anyone attempting to develop interpretive skills and procedures. In order to deal adequately with these human characteristics, we must consider those which apply generally to the entire Bible, as well as those which have particular application to each of the Bible's two major sections, the Old Testament and the New Testament.

### The Inspiration of the Bible

Without any question, the most significant characteristic of the Bible which affects our procedures for interpretation it is that *it is inspired.* The belief that the Bible is inspired has been a major part of Christian faith since the earliest times. It has become even more significant in our own time. This affirmation also serves as the foundation for Christian acceptance of the Bible as authoritative in matters of faith and practice. But to claim that the Bible is inspired is one thing, to understand what each of us means by that statement is quite another. Therefore, let us see if we can reach an agreement upon the actual content of that statement of faith.

## The Meaning of Inspiration

The word *inspiration* actually occurs only twice in the Bible. In the Old Testament Job was told,

> But there is a spirit in man: and the inspiration of the Almighty giveth them understanding (Job 32:8, KJV).

However, this has more recently been translated as,

> But it is the spirit in a man,
>     the breath of the Almighty,
>     that makes him understand (Job 32:8).

The latter translation may be more literal, but it does not significantly change the meaning. In addition to this statement, the New Testament records that

> All scripture is given by inspiration of God, and is profitable for doctrine, for reproof, for correction, for instruction in righteousness (2 Tim. 3:16, KJV).

While the Revised Standard Version is slightly different in its wording of the translation of this verse, its meaning is clearly identical, for there we are told, "All scripture is inspired by God" (2 Tim. 3:16).

In both instances, the terms for inspiration clearly refer to the breath of God. The Old Testament Hebrew expression is "the breath of the Almighty," while the New Testament Greek word is made up of two words which mean "God-breathed." Thus, it is quite clear that the biblical concept of inspiration refers to that which has been breathed into by God.

The idea apparently refers back to the creation account, where we are told:

> Then the Lord God formed man of dust from the ground, and breathed into his nostrils the breath of life; and man became a living being (Gen. 2:7).

This adds the additional dimension to the concept of inspiration that God's breath gives life.

Unfortunately, our contemporary use of the term *inspiration* has become somewhat less specific. We speak of almost anything which stirs our emotions as being inspired. We refer to music, art, poetry, and such things as being inspired. When we use the term this way, we are seldom making any reference to God; we are merely identifying something which touches us emotionally.

In this book, I am going to confine my use of the term *inspiration* to its strictly biblical meaning. It refers to that which has been breathed into by God, to that which has been filled with his breath or Spirit. I am in no way denying the validity of other uses of the term. However, you need clearly to understand that I am using the term in this more technical, theological sense.

However, defining inspiration with precision still does not solve our basic problem. Though we may now be clear about what we mean by inspiration, we still have not set forth an answer to the question, "What do we mean when we say the Bible is inspired?" Admittedly, we mean that the Bible is God-breathed. But what does this mean? We must proceed further in our search for an answer. It appears to me that there are at least three other ideas which must be considered if we are going to answer this question fully.

### The Inspiration of the Writers

First, in trying to come to grips with the biblical understanding of its own inspiration, we must begin with the human authors, those people over the centuries who spoke or wrote the various parts of the Bible. The Second Epistle of Peter bluntly asserts that "men moved by the Holy Spirit spoke from God" (2 Pet. 1:21). Far too often our considerations of biblical inspiration have omitted this dimension. Yet, it appears that this is precisely where the Bible begins.

Any concept of biblical inspiration must go back to those saints, known and unknown, who were directed by God to proclaim and to record his message. It is quite likely that when this concept was written, the only Scripture which was around was the Old Testament. Parts of the New Testament were already written, but much of it was not yet collected. Whether any of it was as yet considered to be authoritative Scripture is problematical. But that is all beside the point. The text says that men were inspired to speak God's word. Whenever or wherever it was spoken or recorded, those who did it were inspired by God, moved by his Spirit. It is that simple. But it is also that profound.

This idea appears to me to be basic. Any discussion of biblical inspiration which does not go back to the human spokesmen doesn't go back far enough. God inspired his people to present and preserve his Word. This is our first affirmation in our statement of the doctrine of biblical inspiration.

### The Inspiration of the Words

But that is only the beginning point. There is a second affirmation which must be added. The key thought here is contained in Paul's admonition to Timothy, "All scripture is inspired by God" (2 Tim. 3:16). Again, it is not of major significance for our basic consideration that when this was written, the Old Testament was probably the only Scripture which was around. Much of the New Testament had most likely not been written, and certainly it had not been canonized, accepted as authoritative. However, the statement ultimately applies to any Scripture, whether it was written before or afterwards.

This affirmation applies to the words themselves. Some have claimed that the reference only applies to the ideas of Scripture. That is quite unlikely, for ideas cannot be communicated without words. Admittedly, people can communicate with the deaf by use of signs. But those are merely substitutes for words. Furthermore, great art can communicate the emotions of the artist, but at best that is only vague, not precise. When it comes down to the bottom line, basic communication requires words. When the Bible affirms that the Scriptures are inspired, it is clearly referring to the words themselves.

In some way, God has breathed life into the very words of the Bible. His Holy Spirit fills them and uses them in giving life to people.

Again, we should note another significant concept. Some would claim that only the original manuscripts were inspired. I am sure that they were. But this assertion points to the Scripture as the early Christians actually had it, not as it was originally written. The Bible as it has come down to us, through the centuries of copying, is also inspired by God. The Bible you and I use is God-breathed. His Spirit gives life and power through it. I have heard God speak through its pages.

So our concept of inspiration now has two basic affirmations. The men who spoke and wrote the Bible were inspired. But the words which they spoke and wrote are inspired as well. God has breathed upon his people through the whole process, not in just one part. It is at this point that most of us stop in our consideration of inspiration. But there is a third affirmation which the Bible makes about inspiration. It is to that which we must now turn.

### The Inspiration of the Interpreters

Our third affirmation concerning the inspiration of the Bible focuses upon us and others who are interpreters of God's Word. The interpreters of Scripture can be inspired.

As we have noted earlier in this chapter, young Elihu castigated the false interpretations set forth by Job and his three friends by saying,

> I said, "Let days speak,
>     and many years teach wisdom."
> But it is the spirit in a man,
>     the breath of the Almighty,
>     that makes him understand.
> It is not the old that are wise,
>     nor the aged that understand what is right (Job 32:7-9).

Here is the plain assertion that wisdom comes through the interpreter being filled with God's Spirit, being breathed upon by God. That is the way to truth.

This idea is underscored by the New Testament's teaching that

> No prophecy of scripture is a matter of one's own interpretation,

> because no prophecy ever came by the impulse of man, but men moved by the Holy Spirit spoke from God (2 Pet. 1:20-21).

With these words we are informed that the same Spirit who moved upon the original speakers also moves upon the interpreters. This also carries the inherent warning that any interpreter who seeks to understand the Scriptures without being led by God's Spirit is doomed to failure. You cannot—you dare not—interpret the Scriptures alone.

Jesus also underscored this point in dealing with his original disciples. In conversation, he made the following two statements.

> These things have I spoken to you, while I am still with you. But the Counselor, the Holy Spirit, whom the Father will send in my name, he will teach you all things, and bring to your remembrance all that I have said to you (John 14:25-26).

> I have many things to say to you, but you cannot bear them now. When the Spirit of truth comes, he will guide you into all the truth (John 16:12-13).

Both of these statements assert that God's Holy Spirit is available and able to guide disciples into truth. This certainly includes their interpretation and understanding of what had already been given to them in the Scriptures. That this is true is indicated by Jesus' command,

> Search the scriptures, because you think in them to have life eternal, and they are what witness to me (John 5:39, author's translation).

So the third affirmation of the biblical concept of inspiration is that God's Spirit is available and seeking to inspire the interpreter. This means that interpretation is a spiritual discipline. It must be undergirded with prayer, asking the guidance of God's Spirit. The interpreter must be open to the leadership of the Holy Spirit.

The biblical teachings concerning the inspiration of the Scriptures can then be summarized by these three statements.

1. The original speakers and writers of the Scriptures were inspired by God.

2. The words which they wrote and which have been passed on to us over the centuries are inspired.

3. The interpreter who approaches the Word of God today can be inspired by the same Spirit who has directed the whole process.

A great deal more could be deduced from a thorough study of the Bible. But that is outside the purpose of this book. Nevertheless, one other area related to the inspiration of the Scriptures should be considered: the process by which the Bible was originally inspired.

## Theories of Inspiration

It is imperative for the interpreter to recognize that there is a difference between the fact of inspiration and theories as to how it occurred. Theories are human attempts to explain known facts. An old story tells of the plight of the mother who noticed that each day when her son came home from kindergarten, his drawings were all done with a black crayon. Becoming deeply disturbed over this, she took him to see a psychiatrist. She wished to know what kind of deep-seated anxieties caused her son to be so depressed and somber. Imagine her reaction when the psychiatrist informed her that the child's drawings were done in black because that was the only crayon he had which was not broken.

The mother had seen the facts of the all-black drawings. But her theory to explain these facts was totally wrong. There was another, simpler theory which explained the same facts. It also happened to be the correct one.

When we approach the Bible, there are several different theories proposed to explain how God inspired it. But the fact remains that he did. Divergent theories do not change the facts. Note, however, that the theories are merely human attempts to explain the known facts. They must never be confused with the facts themselves.

There are three basic theories of inspiration, usually identified as (1) verbal inspiration, (2) plenary (full) inspiration, and (3) dynamic inspiration. These are frequently defined in different ways. However, the more usual definitions are these.

*Verbal* inspiration is usually applied to the Bible in the original languages, as it was originally written, and claims that these writings were so inspired that the very words of Scripture were dictated by God.

_Plenary_ inspiration is usually defined as teaching that the Bible was inspired fully, but that it was not dictated by God, leaving the human authors free to choose their own words to express the divine revelation.

_Dynamic_ inspiration usually is defined as being the powerful process by which God inspired both the writers and the words which they wrote, but without making the writers mere automatons.

We need to be quite aware of the fact that each of these is nothing more than a human theory, attempting to explain or define the process by which God gives his word to us. Such theories may help us come to grips with these facts, but they must never take the place of the facts. Theories may change. Facts will not. Each of these theories has its strengths and its weaknesses. But no one of them appears to be fully satisfactory. It appears to me to be far safer to acknowledge the clear teachings of the Bible concerning its inspiration and to avoid seeking to substitute human theories in their place. (A good discussion of this subject may be found in _The Broadman Bible Commentary_, vol. 1, rev., pp. 5-9, by Clifton J. Allen.)

For our purposes in this book, the following statement appears to be sufficient. The biblical speakers and writers were inspired by God. The words which they wrote and which have come to us were also inspired by God. Finally, the contemporary interpreter may be inspired by the same Spirit as he seeks to understand and interpret the Bible. This is a common characteristic of the whole Bible. But it is this characteristic which makes the Bible unique. It must be taken into consideration by any technique or procedure of interpretation which we develop.

## The Unity and Diversity of the Bible

The second major characteristic of the Bible which must affect our techniques of interpretation is its unity and diversity. This at first sounds quite strange, that the Bible can both be a unity and at the same time be characterized by diversity. However, it is true.

There is a unity within the Bible which has stood the test of time. It is the divine story of redemption, of God working through his people to accomplish his purposes. This common theme runs throughout the Bible. The people of the New Testament looked back to the Old Testament for the roots from which their faith grew. The people of the Old Testament looked forward to the ultimate flowering of their faith. This occurred in Christ Jesus and was recorded in the New Testament. It is this unity of purpose which has demonstrated its divine nature and which has held the Bible together under the onslaughts of the centuries.

At the same time, even the most superficial reading of the Bible points up its great diversity. It is diverse in content. The sacrificial laws of Leviticus are a far cry from the great love chapter of Paul in 1 Corinthians 13. The harsh proclamations of judgment by Amos are far removed from the stories of Jesus in the Gospels. The constant rebellions found in Kings and Chronicles are widely different from the record of the spread of the gospel found in Acts. The Sermon on the Mount is a major leap beyond the Ten Commandments (Matt. 5 to 7; Ex. 20:1-17). This list could be multiplied many times.

Furthermore, not only is the Bible diverse in content, it is also diverse in literary structure. We have some common literary types in both Testaments, such as history and sermons. But the New Testament has no literature comparable to the legal material of the Old. And the Old Testament has no material really comparable to the Gospels and the Epistles of the New.

Any satisfactory technique for interpreting the Bible must take account of the strange features of its unity and diversity. One or the other of these features by itself would offer no great problems. It is the fact that we have both in this one book with which we must adequately deal.

In addition to these characteristics of the Bible which indicate its divine nature, both the Old Testament and the New Testament have human characteristics with which we must also deal in developing a procedure for interpreting the Bible. As we consider these, some of these characteristics will be similar. That similarity is real. But as we probe more deeply, it will become obvious that some of these similar characteristics of the two Testaments have quite different applications in each. Our techniques of interpretation must deal with all of these, both in their similarities and in their divergences.

# 2
# The Human Nature of the Bible

A great deal of literature has survived from the ancient Near East. Among that literature is the collection of books which we know as the Bible. In seeking to develop our techniques for interpreting the Bible, we must consider it against its literary background. As a book of literature, it possesses human characteristics. Some of these human characteristics are shared by one or more other ancient books. Some of these human characteristics are shared, to some degree, by all ancient books. But there are some of these human characteristics, as well as the divine characteristics, which are quite different from other ancient literary works. In developing interpretive procedures, we must consider each of these characteristics, including the common, the uncommon, and the unique. It is the total picture of the Bible which its individual characteristics give us which we must comprehend. Taken together, they will give us an adequate portrayal of the human side of this book which we are seeking to understand.

## The Literature of the Bible

### The Literature of the Old Testament

The Old Testament is not just one book, it is a collection of books. We could actually describe it as the sacred library of ancient Israel. Anyone who seeks to understand and interpret it must be aware of this basic fact. There are actually thirty-nine separate books which are included in it. These were written over hundreds of years and represent many different kinds of literature. There were numerous authors and compilers, each with his individual point of view, his characteristic vocabulary and style, and his unique intellectual ability and spiritual insight. All of these facts must be taken into account by an interpreter.

The Old Testament was divided into three sections by the ancient Hebrews. In their arrangement, the first five books make up the first section, which is called the *Torah* or the "Law." These books are Genesis, Exodus, Leviticus, Numbers, and Deuteronomy. It is immediately obvious to anyone who reads these books that they are noticeably different in form and content from those which make up the second section. That section is called the *Nebhi'im* or the "Prophets." This section is additionally divided into two subsections. The first of these is known as the "Former Prophets," and includes Joshua, Judges, 1 and 2 Samuel, and 1 and 2 Kings. The second subsection is called the "Latter Prophets," and is made up of Isaiah, Jeremiah, Ezekiel, and the twelve (the so-called Minor Prophets). The last section of the Hebrew Bible is known as the *Kethubim* or the "Writings" and includes all of the remaining books. The nature of the material in each of these sections is different from that in the others and, therefore, demands different techniques for interpretation.

Normally, however, contemporary interpreters tend to categorize the literature of the Old Testament somewhat differently. The basic division between individual books as well as between parts of books is usually based upon whether we are dealing with prose or poetry. Prose is generally quite straightforward, while poetry is more frequently an author's attempt to express emotions and ideas which are difficult to put meaningfully into simple words. As an illustration, consider the thought that no one would try to interpret the following two passages in the same way.

> So David went and brought up the ark of God from the house of Obed-edom to the city of David with rejoicing; and when those who bore the ark of the Lord had gone six paces, he sacrificed an ox and a fatling. And David danced before the Lord with all his

might; and David was girded with a linen ephod (2 Sam. 6:12b-14).

The mountains and the hills before you
  shall break forth into singing,
  and all the trees of the field shall clap their hands
  (Isa. 55:12).

Although quite different in content, both passages are expressing exuberant joy and praise before the Lord. The difference lies in the fact that one passage is prose, while the other is poetry. The prose gives details, describes action, and tells a story. The poetry with its rhythm and sweeping images communicates a feeling, appealing to the emotions.

Both the prose and the poetry of the Old Testament, however, may be further subdivided into other categories of literature or literary structure. Prose material may be categorized as simple narrative, sacred history, legal material, speeches, and apocalyptic material, along with several other classifications of lesser significance. Although most of these categories are probably familiar to you in some degree, apocalyptic material may be somewhat strange. Apocalyptic material is visionary and highly symbolic. Examples in the Bible are parts of Daniel in the Old Testament and Revelation in the New Testament, along with a few passages from other books in both Testaments.

Poetry, on the other hand, is divided into hymns, ballads, liturgies, wisdom materials, and sermons, along with a few other minor categories also. Each of these subdivisions of both prose and poetry will usually require slightly different techniques for interpretation. (In some cases, the differences will be more than slight.) The following examples of the various types of prose and poetry will show just how different each of these subdivisions may be and, therefore, why they require different interpretative techniques.

### Prose

*Simple narrative:* So Abram went, as the Lord had told him; and Lot went with him. Abram was seventy-five years old when he departed from Haran (Gen. 12:4).

*Sacred history:* And Ahab the son of Omri did evil in the sight of the Lord more than all that were before him. And as if it had been a light thing for him to walk in the sins of Jeroboam the son of Nebat, he took for wife Jezebel the daughter of Ethbaal king of the Sidonians, and went and served Baal, and worshiped him (1 Kings 16:30-31).

*Legal material:* You shall have no other gods before me (Ex. 20:3).

*Speech:* And Elijah came near to all the people, and said, "How long will you go limping with two different opinions? If the Lord is God, follow him; but if Baal, then follow him" (1 Kings 18:21).

*Apocalyptic:* And four great beasts came up out of the sea, different from one another. The first was like a lion and had eagles' wings. Then as I looked its wings were plucked off, and it was lifted up from the ground and made to stand upon two feet like a man; and the mind of a man was given to it (Dan. 7:3-4).

### Poetry

*Hymn:*   The heavens are telling the glory of God;
    and the firmament proclaims his handiwork.
Day to day pours forth speech,
    and night to night declares knowledge.
There is no speech, nor are there words;
    their voice is not heard;
yet their voice goes out through all the earth,
    and their words to the end of the world (Ps. 19:1-4).

*Ballad:*   Let me sing for my beloved
    a love song concerning his vineyard:
My beloved had a vineyard
    on a very fertile hill (Isa. 5:1).

*Liturgy:*   Lift up your heads, O gates!
    and be lifted up, O ancient doors!
    that the King of glory may come in.
Who is the King of glory?
    The Lord, strong and mighty,
    the Lord, mighty in battle! (Ps. 24:7-8).

*Wisdom:*   Three things are never satisfied;
    four never say, "Enough":
Sheol, the barren womb,

> the earth ever thirsty for water,
> and the fire which never says, "Enough"
> (Prov. 30:15b-16).

*Sermon:* Hear, O heavens, and give ear, O earth;
>        for the Lord has spoken:
> "Sons I have reared and brought up,
>        but they have rebelled against me.
> The ox knows its owner,
>        and the ass its master's crib;
> but Israel does not know,
>        my people does not understand" (Isa. 1:2-3).

When considering these examples of various literary types from the Old Testament, it is obvious that no one technique of interpretation could possibly be adequate for dealing with all of these. Each book, then, must be identified as to its basic nature. Each passage must be considered in the light of its individual literary characteristics. There is simply no other way to get the job done.

### The Literature of the New Testament

The literary problems of the New Testament are somewhat different from those of the Old Testament. The New Testament, also, is a collection of books. It was the sacred library of the early churches. It is actually made up of twenty-seven books, many with distinctive literary characteristics.

Dividing passages into prose and poetry is not particularly useful for the New Testament interpreter. There are small amounts of poetry in the New Testament, generally reflecting either ancient hymns or quotations from poetic portions of the Old Testament. While these need to be handled a bit differently from prose passages, they are relatively few in number and, therefore, in significance, when compared with the prose sections of the New Testament. On the other hand, the more traditional classification of the New Testament materials into Gospels, history, Epistles, and apocalyptic can be quite helpful as a beginning step for the interpreter. However, these kinds of literature must be clearly defined and understood.

The Gospels consist of Matthew, Mark, Luke, and John. They actually represent a kind of literature unique to the Christian tradition. They are not biographies, for they do not in any way seek to tell the life of Jesus. Large blocks of time in his life are skipped over totally. Only two Gospels record his birth, and, other than his visit to the Temple as a boy (Luke 2:44-52), nothing is told of the period between his early infancy and his baptism. Furthermore, the things which are recorded cover only scattered events from Jesus' baptism to the week of his passion. These books consist of what might better be called sacred history. It is the record of the early Christians' memories of Jesus. The events selected were not an attempt to record his life but to interpret his ministry and mission to all men. They are primarily a record of what God was doing in that time, a statement of the good news that "in Christ God was reconciling the world to himself" (2 Cor. 5:19). The word *gospel* literally means *good news*. It was to communicate this good news that the Gospels were written.

> Now Jesus did many other signs in the presence of the disciples, which are not written in this book; but these are written that you may believe that Jesus is the Christ, the Son of God, and that believing you may have life in his name (John 20:30-31).

Gospel material, then, must not be handled either as simple history or as simple biography. It must be recognized as a theological statement, presenting the words and deeds of Jesus as a means to the end of stating both evangelically and redemptively what God did in Christ and what this means for all people.

The second type of literature in the New Testament has frequently been called history, and it is found in Acts. Here, too, a better literary category would be sacred history. The Book of Acts in no way records history as we understand the term in a contemporary setting. Here, too, the material is presented as a record of what God was doing by his Holy Spirit through the early Christians and their churches. It must be interpreted as a theological statement about God's activities rather than as a historical statement about human history. An interpreter should never forget this.

The Epistles, on the other hand, are ancient letters, which appear to fall into three basic categories. These twenty-one letters, extending from Romans through Jude, may be understood simply as personal letters (Philemon, 2 Timothy, Titus, and 2 and 3 John), church letters, addressed to a specific historical crisis (1 and 2 Corinthians, Galatians, Philippians, Colossians, 1 and 2 Thessalonians, James, 1 and 2 Peter, 1 John, and Jude), and semitheological essays (Romans, Ephesians, 1 Timothy, and Hebrews).

Epistles must generally be handled differently from other types of literature. It was apparently assumed that each would be read from beginning to end at one time. (Letters are not normally read one sentence or one paragraph at a time. You may go back and ponder them in this way, but you usually read them all at once.) Further, letters addressed to specific historical crises must be understood against the background of these crises. In the same manner, letters which are strictly personal must be understood against the background of the relationship which existed between the writer and the addressee. Even letters which are semitheological essays must be understood in the light of the theological and historical situations which produced them and to which they were addressed.

The fourth literary category of the New Testament is apocalyptic. The basic book of this type is the Revelation, although there are a few other scattered passages which might be so described. Apocalyptic literature is usually highly symbolic, with emphasis upon visions and bold, strange imagery. It is intensely practical in purpose, addressed to a present audience, although it makes predictions of the future. Any attempt to interpret such material in a manner which ignores these characteristics will miss the basic emphasis.

In summary, the interpreter of the New Testament does not have nearly as many literary categories to confront as does the Old Testament interpreter. But it should be obvious that the following passages require different techniques in arriving at their interpretation.

## Gospel

Jesus said to him, "I am the way, and the truth, and the life; no one comes to the Father, but by me. If you had known me, you would have known my Father also; henceforth you know him and have seen him" (John 14:6-7).

## Sacred History

And day by day, attending the temple together and breaking bread in their homes, they partook of food with glad and generous hearts, praising God and having favor with all the people. And the Lord added to their number day by day those who were being saved (Acts 2:46-47).

## Epistle

*Personal:* I appeal to you for my child, Onesimus, whose father I have become in my imprisonment. . . . I am sending him back to you, sending my very heart (Philem. 10-12).

*Church:* I am astonished that you are so quickly deserting him who called you in the grace of Christ and turning to a different gospel—not that there is another gospel, but there are some who trouble you and want to pervert the gospel of Christ (Gal. 1:6-7).

*Semitheological essay:* And every priest stands daily at his service, offering repeatedly the same sacrifices, which can never take away sins. But when Christ had offered for all time a single sacrifice for sins, he sat down at the right hand of God (Heb. 10:11-12).

## Apocalyptic

Then I saw a new heaven and a new earth; for the first heaven and the first earth had passed away, and the sea was no more. And I saw the holy city, new Jerusalem, coming down out of heaven from God, prepared as a bride adorned for her husband (Rev. 21:1-2).

As in the Old Testament, it is obvious that no one technique of interpretation can handle each of the literary categories illustrated above. The interpreter must begin by identifying the literary type and then must develop and utilize a procedure appropriate to that type. Each book and each passage must be dealt with according to its own literary type. Anything less is less than our best.

The Antiquity of the Bible

## The Antiquity of the Old Testament

The interpreter must also recognize that the Old Testament is not only a collection of books representing diverse kinds of literature, it is a collection of ancient books. Although we cannot date the actual time of writing of the books in the Old Testament, their writing certainly extended from at least 1250 BC to about 167 BC. In addition, much of its contents were in a relatively fixed oral form long before they were written. This means that the modern interpreter is separated from any particular passage by at least two thousand years and from many passages by considerably more than three thousand years. It was a significantly different world which produced the Old Testament than that in which we live. We have difficulty in understanding what was going on in our own land in the period of the Civil War (AD 1860-1864), which was only a little more than a century ago. How much more difficult is it for us to bridge a gap of understanding which extends for more than two millennia?

The pages of the Old Testament are filled with unfamiliar peoples and nations, such as Assyria, Syria, Babylon, the Philistines, the Hittites, the Girgashites, and the Midianites. Those people had strange names, such as Raamses, Sennacherib, Merodach-baladan, Tiglath-pileser, and Maher-shalal-hashbaz. These are difficult to pronounce and more difficult to remember or to understand. Yet, if these peoples' names are difficult, how much more difficult is it for us to bridge the gap between their world and ours? However, it must be done if we are going to understand and interpret the Old Testament. Its very antiquity gives major problems to us as we seek to interpret it.

To illustrate this difficulty, consider the relatively insignificant problem of ancient weights and measures. Length was measured in cubits and spans. Weights were measured in talents, minas, and shekels. Volume was measured in homers, lethechs, ephahs, baths, and kabs. Not only do we have difficulty in arriving at precise contemporary figures for understanding these terms, we must first of all seek to discover if the same system was used throughout the Old Testament period and if it was consistent in its meaning during that time. For example, the interpreter must know if shekel was used as a measurement for weight for the entire Old Testament era, and, if it was, did it refer to the exact same weight in 1200 BC as it did in 400 BC? It is highly probable that the meaning of these terms varied from the beginning to the end of the Old Testament period. It is also probable that while some terms were used throughout the entire period, others were not. But the interpreter must seek to know these things in order to accurately understand the biblical message. If this is true of such minor things as weights and measures, how much more true is it of key theological words? The gap of the centuries must be bridged, as best we can. The better we bridge it, the better we will be able to understand the message of these ancient books.

### The Antiquity of the New Testament

The New Testament, like the Old Testament, is also a collection of ancient books. However, the New Testament writings and the events which they record cover a much more limited period. It is highly probable that the books of the New Testament were written in a period of less than a century. The events which are recorded in it certainly cover less than this. Therefore, the history which the interpreter needs to master is far more restricted than that of the Old Testament era.

On the other hand, it is still a period which is far removed from us. The people who move across the pages of the New Testament are still quite foreign to us in name, in culture, in language, and in thought patterns. Their daily practices, their forms of government, and their style of living are very unfamiliar to us, no matter how much we have studied the Bible. However, since most Christians have focused far more time and study on the New Testament than on the Old, its historical period does not seem quite so foreign to most of us. But we must beware of assuming that because we are more familiar with the New Testament that we know all (or even most) of what we need to know about its backgrounds.

As an example of this, consider the events of the last twenty-four hours of Jesus' earthly life. In spite of the extreme familiarity of these events to most Christians, consider how little we actually know about the real background. The nature and function of the high priest at that time was different even from his functions in late Old Testament times, and there is not even one single person in our world who has even the most remote similarity to his function. Further, what do you really know about the organization and responsibilities of the Sanhedrin, or of a Roman procurator? And how do these relate to Herod Antipas, to whom Pilate sent Jesus? Furthermore, what do you really know about the nature of a Roman crucifixion? These questions represent only a few of the many which can be raised about the historical background of one event in the New Testament. Both the events and the questions can and should be multiplied. You and I as interpreters must do our very best to span this gap of the centuries. Our effectiveness in doing this will enhance our understanding of the events and determine to some degree our effectiveness as interpreters. Ancient books must be understood against their ancient backgrounds. To ignore their antiquity is to run the risk of major misinterpretations.

## The Languages of the Bible

### The Languages of the Old Testament

Most of the Old Testament was written in Hebrew, with a very small part in Aramaic. (The Aramaic sections are Dan. 2:4*b* to 7:28; Ezra 4:8 to 6:18; 7:12-26; and Jer. 10:11.) Biblical Aramaic is descended from Hebrew and is similar to it in form and structure. Both are in the Semitic family of languages and are quite different in grammar and syntax from English. It is extremely difficult for us to enter into the ancient thought patterns of these languages, but it is absolutely necessary that we make the attempt. There are several major differences between Hebrew and English which *must be understood* if we are going to interpret the Old Testament properly.

The first characteristic of Hebrew with which we must become familiar is its emphasis upon action. The verb is the key word in Israel's language. The ancient Hebrews did not involve themselves much with philosophical or theological language as we understand those terms. Rather, they were far more concerned with reporting what God did than with describing what God was like. This fact is important in any attempt to understand and interpret the faith of the Old Testament. Those ancient Hebrews would never have spoken of "the biblical doctrine of election." Rather, they told and retold the story of how God had chosen them, delivering them from slavery in Egypt. This account was retold every time they celebrated the festival of Passover (Ex. 12:24-27). This emphasis upon what God had done served as the foundation for their understanding of God as living and active. The Old Testament is a record of action, not a summary exposition of a theological system.

A second significant characteristic of the Hebrew language with which we must become familiar is the fact that Hebrew verbs do not have any time concept in their forms, such as those with which we are familiar in English. There is no past, present, or future tense in Hebrew. Rather, their verbs describe the *state* of an action. The two basic states of action indicated by Hebrew verbs are complete and incomplete. The Hebrews could even describe events in the future as completed action, because it was completed in the mind of God. As an illustration, consider this popular messianic prophecy:

> For to us a child is born,
>     to us a son is given (Isa. 9:6a).

Both verbs in this verse describe the action as already completed, though the event was apparently in the future.

In addition, the change from one kind of action to another can be significant. This verse goes on to say, "and the government will be upon his shoulder." Here, a verb form was used which shows incomplete action. The coming child would be born. But that was an action which would happen once and be finished, completed. However, after his birth, God would place the divine authority upon him and that would never be completed. This God-given government of the kingdom would always be upon him. He would always have this authority. Thus, in interpreting the Old Testament, we need to recognize this quality of their verbs. Just as significant for interpretation, we must also recognize that *the time setting of any action is revealed solely by the context.* An interpreter forgets this at his peril. We must constantly be looking for clues as to the time of any particular action.

Finally, words in ancient Hebrew do not necessarily have the same meaning as words in our language. We must be careful that we use words in the same sense as they did. Consider the use of the word *perfect* in the following passages.

> Noah was a just man and perfect in his generations (Gen. 6:9, KJV).

> Hast thou considered my servant Job, that there is none like him in the earth, a perfect and upright man, one that feareth God, and escheweth evil? (Job 1:8, KJV).

To us, as we read such a passage, *perfect* means morally upright, sinless. But to the ancient Hebrews, the word actually meant "complete," "finished." These statements referring to Noah and to Job did not refer to their morality but to their maturity. They were being described as spiritually mature. They may or may not have been morally upright, but that has to be determined elsewhere. This word says nothing about it. From these illustrations, it becomes readily apparent that the fact that the Old Testament was written in Hebrew (and Aramaic) is of great significance for any interpreter. If we fail to understand either words or actions, we may grossly misunderstand a verse.

## The Language of the New Testament

The New Testament was written in Greek. This, however, was not the Greek language in which the great classics of ancient Greece were written. The Greek of the New Testament was written in the _koine_ (pronounced as _coin-ay_) or common language. This was the language of the ordinary people in the New Testament era. It was the language of the marketplace.

The _koine_ Greek is much more similar to English in structure and thought patterns than the language of the Old Testament is. On the other hand, it is still a foreign language and has both numerous and significant differences from our own. Furthermore, since most (if not all) of the writers of the New Testament spoke Aramaic as their basic language as first-century Jews, the Greek of the New Testament does have a decided Semitic tone. Frequently, sentences and phrases are apparently used with a significant emphasis upon an Aramaic thought pattern.

While there is not as much difficulty for an interpreter to grasp Greek sentence structure and/or word meanings as there was with the Hebrew, there are still problems. Many words just do not translate precisely into English. There are some verb forms which do not have any parallel. However, our knowledge of Greek is so much better than our knowledge of Hebrew that we can feel a great deal more confidence in the translations.

We need to be aware that an interpreter can usually approach modern translations with confidence. (These will be discussed in detail in chapter 4, "Tools for Interpreting the Bible.") On the other hand, a knowledge of the original language is a major help. Perhaps we need to be reminded, however, that a knowledge of the original language does not automatically ensure a correct interpretation. If it did, all those who know the original languages would agree. It is obvious that this is not so.

The interpreter who does not know the original language, however, at least needs to be aware that translation from one language to another is an inexact science. But there are certain characteristics of these ancient languages which we should know and be able to apply as we seek to interpret any biblical text. If we do not know these, then good commentaries can help fill in this gap in our knowledge.

## The Cultural Background of the Bible

### *The Culture of the Old Testament*

Related both to the antiquity and to the language of the Old Testament, the culture from which it sprang is also very significant for interpretation. Further, since the period which the Old Testament covers is so long and its territory so broad, the changes in culture from era to era and from place to place are also of importance.

To understand the patriarchal narratives of Genesis, for example, we must know something of their cultural background. Knowing the significance they attached to the spoken word is absolutely essential for grasping the meaning of Jacob's theft of the blessing which belonged to Esau (Gen. 27:27-33). To us in our day, it would appear simple for Isaac to have gone ahead and blessed Esau, denying the blessing to Jacob; especially since Jacob had gotten the blessing through deceit. But those ancient people believed that words, once spoken, possessed a power which could not be recalled. Thus, spoken words were absolutely binding. This fact makes real sense out of the whole episode.

Furthermore, since the Old Testament not only covers so much time, but so much territory as well, the culture of each of the nations from Egypt to Babylon is also important. The command, "You shall not boil a kid in its mother's milk" (Ex. 23:19*b*), was once interpreted as a prohibition based upon humane concerns. It seemed to be the utmost in cruelty to boil a kid in its mother's milk. But we now know that boiling a kid in its mother's milk was a means of worshiping the god Chemosh in the land of Moab. Thus this commandment was a prohibition against participating in Moabite worship or in anything which might appear to be Moabite worship. It was a demand for absolute loyalty to God. Further, the statement in Deuteronomy 11:10 about the Hebrews in Egypt watering the land with their feet appears to be absolutely nonsensical at first glance. However, when we realize that slaves in Egypt pedaled a bicycle-like contraption which turned a waterwheel which in turn lifted water from canals to irrigate the land, the passage makes sense. It was a clear reference to Israel's time of servitude in Egypt. In such ways, knowing the cultural background of the Old Testament becomes extremely important to those of us who would interpret its message.

## The Culture of the New Testament

The cultural background of the New Testament is equally as important for its interpretation as is that of the Old Testament. Again, due to the briefer time span with which the New Testament deals, the cultural background is far more limited. On the other hand, its geographical focus is much broader.

The immediate background out of which Palestinian Christianity arose is Greek, Roman, and Hebraic. The Greek influence reigned supreme over that region from the time of Alexander (333 BC). Even the Maccabean revolt of 168 BC and the Roman conquest under Pompey in 63 BC only modified the Greek civilization which had spread over the world. At the same time, during this period the religion and faith of the Old Testament were being transformed into first-century Judaism, with its Pharisees, Sadducees, and Essenes, and with the growing importance of the synagogue as the center of its worship.

All of these must be understood in order to place early Christianity against its proper background. We must also recognize that Christianity was not confined to Palestine. The persecutions and the missionary activities of the first century caused Christianity to spread quickly from this outlying province of the empire to its very heart, Rome. Again, we must come to grips with the variety of cultures which those early witnesses faced and to which and from which they ministered. The Corinthian correspondence loses a great deal of its impact when we do not know the cultural background of Corinth. Paul's experiences in Athens become rather prosaic unless we understand the culture of Athens in his day. And the entire sequence of events following his arrest and ultimate journey to Rome is difficult to comprehend unless we understand the Roman legal system. Any ancient book becomes much more meaningful when we grasp its cultural background and impact. The same is true of the books of the Bible, both Old and New Testaments.

## The Religion and Faith of the Bible

### *The Religion and Faith of the Old Testament*

The Old Testament was both the product of and the central guide for the religion and faith of the Hebrew people. The religious rituals and observances which it sets forth are completely foreign to most people of the contemporary world. The primary obstacle to our understanding lies in the fact that we do not have a sacrificial system. Passages which place so much emphasis upon the proper handling of the blood of a sacrificial animal are generally far beyond our comprehension. We would have great difficulty in finding anything meaningful in splashing an animal's blood over a worshiping congregation. The very idea that the odor of the burning flesh of an animal created a worshipful atmosphere staggers our imagination. It is obvious that gaining both an understanding of and an appreciation for their attitude toward sacrifice is a major barrier to us as interpreters.

Furthermore, the entire structure of the Levitical priesthood is generally outside the bounds of our knowledge and understanding. The changing functions of the Levites from the earliest days of the nation to the end of the Old Testament era is also generally unfamiliar to us. Neither do most of us really understand the nature of the Old Testament prophets and their role in Israel's worship personnel.

The paraphernalia and places of Israel's worship are also difficult for us to understand. Further, passages describing their joy in going to the Temple give problems in understanding to any person who gives serious thought to it.

> I was glad when they said to me,
> "Let us go to the house of the Lord!" (Ps. 122:1).

This outcry of the psalmist becomes especially hard to understand when we remember that the Temple was filled with all the sounds of bleating sheep, lowing cattle, and the cries of sacrificial victims, as well as the smell of the slaughterhouse and the odor of burning flesh. The emphasis placed upon the minute details of the altar, the tables, and the fixtures is still more difficult for us to understand.

Finally, the emphasis placed upon religious festivals with their confusing rituals and purposes also becomes a barrier to our understanding. If we have grown up in a church with a Sunday School, we are probably somewhat familiar with Passover. But Tabernacles (or Booths), Pentecost, and Purim become increasingly less familiar. And New Moon and Sheepshearing just about extend outside the limits of our knowledge and understanding. Yet, each of these at one time or another were important to the religion and faith of Israel, and thus of the Old Testament. We must understand and appreciate them if we are to understand and interpret it.

### The Religion and Faith of the New Testament

The religion and faith of the New Testament are far more familiar to most Christians than that of the Old. The reason for this is obvious: We are New Testament Christians. Most contemporary Christians are, at least superficially, followers of the teachings of the New Testament.

This, however, can be both a help and a hindrance to the interpreter's task. It can be a help, for we are generally familiar with the basic message and faith of the New Testament. It can be a hindrance, however, for our very familiarity can lead us to believe that we know more about the faith of the New Testament and the worshiping communities from which it grew than we really do.

For example, we need to remind ourselves that the central figures of the New Testament were the products of first-century Judaism. Jesus was a Jew. He worshiped in a synagogue. Most of the people to whom he ministered and all of his first disciples were Jews, whose faith was initially that of their contemporaries. Paul was a rabbi and a Pharisee. His training had prepared him to be a leader of first-century Judaism, not a Christian missionary or theologian. It is as we recognize this background to the faith of the New Testament that much of its teachings take on new significance. Both the similarities and the differences between early Christianity and first-century Judaism add real depth to our understanding of the New Testament faith. For example, to hear Jesus describe himself as the "Son of man" is almost meaningless until we know what that title meant in first-century Judaism. Then it takes on a richness and a significance which we might easily miss otherwise.

Furthermore, there is a common strand to the faith of both the Old and the New Testaments. The Old Testament was preserved by the early Christians because they dared to believe that Jesus was its fulfillment. They also dared to believe that, as Jesus' followers, they had become heirs to the promises of God in the Old Testament. It is this commonality between the Testaments which binds them together. The New Testament is the flower which grew from the Old Testament's roots. The Old Testament was the only Scripture which the earliest Christians had. In it they found the texts from which they proclaimed the good news of Jesus.

## The Historical Backgrounds of the Bible

### The Historical Background of the Old Testament

We have already noted the Old Testament's emphasis upon action in our consideration of the Old Testament's language. This emphasis carries over into its basic outlook. Since action was important, history was important, for that is where action takes place. Yet we must recognize that history was important to the Hebrews for reasons different from those which make it important to us. The Old Testament is plainly set against a historical background, but it is not just a book of history. The Israelites were not merely interested in what had happened, but in the meaning of what had happened. Consider, for example, the situation of two kings of Israel, Omri and his son Ahab. Omri was such an important king that Assyria long remembered him, calling the Northern Kingdom "the land of Omri." Yet the Book of Kings covers Omri's reign in just eight verses (1 Kings 16:21-28). Ahab, on the other hand, seems to have made a much lesser impact upon the world, yet the Old Testament gives 209 verses to his reign (1 Kings 16:29 to 22:40). The question arises as to why this is so. The answer does not lie in Ahab's or Omri's relative importance, but in the fact that God was doing something of importance in the reign of Ahab. That period had more meaning for Israel since there was a prophet named Elijah on the scene during Ahab's reign. Thus the history which the Old Testament records is not history as we think of it, but "sacred history," history with a divine significance. It is a history of what God was doing, not a history of what man was about.

In order to understand this sacred history, we need to know as much as possible of the history of the entire Old Testament era. This means that we must come to grips with the history of Egypt, Philistia, Canaan, Phoenicia, Syria, Assyria, Babylon, and Persia, to list only the major nations and peoples. We must know their strengths and weaknesses, their times of conquest and their times of defeat. We need also to understand the geography of their lands and of Israel and how this affected their history. For example, during the times of the separated Hebrew kingdoms, Israel was constantly under attack or pressure from without, while Judah was seldom under such pressure. A look at any good historical geography of the region offers an immediate explanation, for the major highways connecting the Mesopotamian Valley with the Nile Valley all passed through Israel, while only a relatively minor highway passed through Judah. Thus Israel was of significance for the passage of trade caravans and of armies; Judah was not.

Further, a knowledge of the changing fortunes of men and nations is absolutely essential for the proper understanding of the history within the Old Testament, and thus of the Old Testament itself. Consider, for example, the nation of Edom. We must know its history in order to understand the information given in Numbers 20:14-21. There have been two different approaches made to the dating the Hebrews' Exodus from Egypt. Some interpreters have dated it in the fifteenth century BC, while others have dated it in the thirteenth century. But archaeological investigation has revealed that Edom, as a nation, was not even in existence in the fifteenth century BC, while in the thirteenth century it was an existing nation with its borders strongly fortified. In the fifteenth century, Moses would not have had to ask permission to lead his people through the land. They could have marched on unhindered. But the Edomite history of the thirteenth century makes his request and subsequent detour around Edom understandable.

## The Historical Background of the New Testament

As we have noted in other areas, the historical background of the New Testament is limited when contrasted to that of the Old Testament. But it is no less important for a proper understanding of that collection of books. Further, we dare not limit our historical considerations just to the period which produced Christianity and its basic documents, the New Testament.

Although world history was generally stable during the formative years of Christianity, there were significant upheavals in the periods immediately prior to the life of Jesus and the early years of Christianity. The Greek conquest of the ancient world, the Maccabean revolt, and the Roman conquest of Syria-Palestine all played a part in establishing the world conditions in which Jesus was born and to which he ministered. To try to understand fully the spread of Christianity without knowing both the events of the centuries which preceded it, as well as the period which actually produced the New Testament, is to work with a serious handicap. We can grasp something of the struggle which went on in Pilate's mind when he was seeking to release Jesus and heard the taunt, "If you release this man, you are not Caesar's friend," (John 19:12). But knowing that there was a specific title presented by Caesar to loyal and meritorious servants, "Friend of Caesar" (Amicus Caesaris), adds a new historical dimension to the threat. One man was stripped of this title just a few years earlier. There followed such a wave of hostility and embarrassment that the man found life impossible and shortly committed suicide. This threat to Pilate then was more than simply that he would be acting in a way unfriendly to Caesar. It was a real threat that he might lose everything if he freed Jesus. This kind of historical background adds a new dimension to our understanding. The historical background adds depth and breadth to the books of the New Testament.

## The Pre-Christian Outlook of the Old Testament

If we did not already know otherwise, a very cursory reading of the Old Testament reveals that it is a pre-Christian book. Its emphasis upon law is strange to those of us who have been brought up with the New Testament emphasis upon grace. Further, the famous *lex talionis* (Law of Retaliation) gives us problems. There Israel was told,

> When a man causes a disfigurement in his neighbor, as he has done it shall be done to him, fracture for fracture, eye for eye, tooth for tooth; as he has disfigured a man, he shall be disfigured (Lev. 24:19-20).

What a far cry this is from Jesus' statement that

> If anyone strikes you on the right cheek, turn to him the other also: . . . and if anyone forces you to go one mile, go with him two miles (Matt. 5:39-41).

Our immediate reaction is to judge the Old Testament's teaching as being harsh and legalistic. But, in its own time, this was given as a prohibition against vengeance. Nothing more than justice could be demanded by a person who had been wronged. Be that as it may, however, the Old Testament is clearly a pre-Christian book with pre-Christian demands and expectations.

Although the Old Testament has a very clear understanding of sin, salvation, and other so-called basic doctrines, these are always roots from which the full-blown New Testament concepts grew. This should not be surprising. If the Old Testament had contained the full revelation of God, we should not have needed the New Testament. On the other hand, to try to understand the basic teachings of the New Testament without a knowledge of how they grew and developed throughout the Old Testament period is pure folly. It is like trying to understand a house by looking only at the roof. At the same time, because the Old Testament is a pre-Christian book, we frequently find it difficult to understand. The harshness of the holy wars described in the Books of Deuteronomy and Joshua has often caused interpreters to reject the Old Testament completely. Its very pre-Christian nature thus frequently becomes a stumbling block to interpretation.

## The Backward Look of the New Testament

The interpreter must also face the fact that the very reason that modern Christians have an Old Testament to interpret is that it was treasured by the early Christians. It was the only Bible which they possessed for many years. They preserved it, not because it told them from whence they had come, but because in it they found passages pointing to Jesus. He was seen and understood as its fulfillment. Jesus himself used it to proclaim his own ministry. Following his baptism, Jesus went to the synagogue in Nazareth and read Isaiah 61:1-2 as the introduction to his ministry (Luke 4:16-21). He also referred to Jeremiah's promise of the New Covenant when he gave an explanation of his ministry to his disciples on the night he was betrayed (Jer. 31:31-34; Matt. 26:28; Mark 14:24). After his resurrection, Jesus explained what had happened by "beginning with Moses and all the prophets" and interpreting to his disciples "in all the scriptures the things concerning himself" (Luke 24:27). The Book of Acts is filled with examples of how the early disciples did precisely the same thing with the Old Testament as they proclaimed Jesus to the world.

Therefore, we must face the fact that the Old Testament was preserved for us by the early Christians. It was a Christian book. It still is. They kept it, not because they were conservative, trying to hold onto their past, but because they were daring. They dared to believe that it was the beginning of the story of God's work of redemption which had been completed with the life, death, and resurrection of Jesus Christ.

## The Forward Look of the Bible

Although the Old Testament is a book firmly rooted and anchored in its own historical times, it also has a distinctly forward look. We must never forget that the prophets spoke to the people of their own day, but they also looked to the future. They often pointed to historical judgments coming in their future, seeking to draw their people back to God so that they might escape the imminent consequences of their sins. They also looked forward to future deliverances from the judgments they were undergoing. It was from both standpoints (God could use history both to punish and deliver) that the prophets proclaimed God's sovereignty over nature and history.

We have also seen that the early Christians believed that the Old Testament looked forward to the coming of God's Messiah. The prophets had glimpsed something of the ultimate fulfillment of God's redemptive purposes in Jesus. But we must also face the fact that from our standpoint in history, many of the things to which the Old Testament looked forward have already occurred. Much of what was future to them is past to us. The interpreter must remember this as he approaches the Old Testament. On the other hand, all that has happened in the processes of history has not exhausted the future look of the Old Testament. The Old Testament most certainly looked forward to some events of both deliverance and of judgment which have not yet occurred. This, too, must be kept in mind by anyone who would interpret the Old Testament. The fact that some of what was future to them is past to us while other is still future adds yet another problem to the task of the Old Testament interpreter. For example, the promised Messiah has come, but elements of his ministry are still to be fulfilled (see Isa. 11).

The New Testament also has a forward look. We must note, however, that its basic message was to the people who lived in that day. Because the old story was addressed to real people in real life, it is still relevant to us who face real life today. But we must not forget or ignore the fact that the New Testament also had a forward look. Rooted and grounded in the absolute sovereignty of God, the people of the New Testament looked forward to the return of Jesus and to the full establishment of his kingdom with new heavens and a new earth.

While the details of the future hope of the early Christians can be passed over at this point in this book, the fact of that hope cannot. If there was one thing of which those early saints were certain, it was that the end of their story was yet to be worked out by God in his sovereign power. The final consummation of the ages was that for which they both longed and looked. It is emphasized throughout the New Testament. A contemporary interpreter must deal with the biblical message in the light of its ultimate hope for the future.

## The Demands of the Bible

The Old Testament made demands upon the people of its day. It still makes demands upon us. The prophets who preached God's judgment and wrath expected a response from their people. There was always a "so what?" to their messages. There still is.

As we approach the Old Testament, we must constantly be seeking for the response which it demands of us. The response which is expected in some places is more difficult to discover than in others. Consider the following passages from Isaiah, for example.

> Bring no more vain offerings;
>    incense is an abomination to me.
> New moon and sabbath and the calling of assemblies—
>    I cannot endure iniquity and solemn assembly.
> Your new moons and your appointed feasts
>    my soul hates;
> They have become a burden to me,
>    I am weary of bearing them (Isa. 1:13-14).
>
> Wash yourselves; make yourselves clean;
>    remove the evil of your doings
>    from before my eyes;
> cease to do evil,
>    learn to do good;
> seek justice,
>    correct oppression;

defend the fatherless,
    plead for the widow (Isa. 1:16-17).

While we may not at all grasp what God expected in the first passage, there is little question about what is expected in the second. The demand for practical righteousness is clearly apparent.

Many of the demands of the Old Testament are also to be found in the legal material. The laws regarding slavery immediately offer us problems (Ex. 21:1-6). But no one has much difficulty grasping what is expected by: "You shall not commit adultery" (Ex. 20:14). Whether clearly obvious or relatively unclear, the fact remains that the Old Testament made demands which expected response. The task of the interpreter is to discover and to understand just what kind of response is demanded.

If this emphasis upon demand and response is true of the Old Testament, it is even more so of the New. Jesus not only expected people to respond to him, he demanded a response. Not content merely to ask them what men were saying of him, he demanded of them, "But who do you say that I am?" (Matt. 16:15). At the conclusion of the parable of the good Samaritan, as soon as the lawyer identified the one who had acted like a neighbor, Jesus commanded, "Go and do likewise" (Luke 10:37). The missionary imperatives, the demands for both righteousness and love in relationships, and the expectations of obedience on the part of Christians are found throughout the New Testament.

The interpreter who fails to come to grips with the demanding nature of the entire Bible has failed to come to grips with its basic message. God offers his love, but he demands response.

It is against this background of both the divine and human nature of the Bible that the interpreter must work. We must approach it from both standpoints if we are to approach it rightly. We now come face to face with the task of the interpreter.

# 3
# The Task of the Interpreter

When driving in strange and unfamiliar territory, I am frequently confronted with road signs which confuse me. It is normally easy to know what they say, but can be another thing to know what they mean. Most of us have been in similar situations. Usually, the best solution is to stop and ask for directions from someone who is familiar with the territory. When the road signs leave us confused, we need an interpreter or a guide.

The same sort of thing arises in biblical study. In order to understand a difficult passage or an unclear verse, we need an interpreter. This is not a new situation. It has been around at least as long as the New Testament era. The Book of Acts records Philip's experience with the Ethiopian eunuch, reading from the Book of Isaiah. There we are told,

> Philip ran to him, . . . and asked, "Do you understand what you are reading?" And he said, "How can I, unless someone guides me?" (Acts 8:30-31).

The Ethiopian needed an interpreter. A similar experience was faced by two disciples of Jesus, walking toward Emmaus after the resurrection of Jesus (Luke 24). They did not understand the relationship between the Old Testament Scriptures and the events of that first Easter morning. When the resurrected Christ approached them and sensed their confusion,

> Beginning with Moses and all the prophets, he interpreted to them in all the scriptures the things concerning himself (Luke 24:27).

Our problem, however, is compounded beyond these two illustrations. Not only do we need an interpreter to help us understand the Scriptures, we ourselves are to be interpreters to others. It is our task to guide them, to make the meaning of this divine-human book clear. God calls his people to be interpreters of his written Word. If we are going to do it, we should do it well. But if we are going to do it well, we must clearly understand what our task is and why it is important.

## The Authority of the Bible

It is necessary for anyone who takes the task of interpretation seriously to come to an understanding of the authority of the Bible. Most Christians agree that the Bible has an authority over life. But it is one thing to believe that the Bible is authoritative and another to define what the nature of that authority is. It is unlikely that we shall be able to arrive at a definition with which all Christians will agree. However, it does appear that there are some basic ideas about the Bible's authority which are common ground and upon which we can build.

First, the Bible is authoritative because it is inspired by God. As I have noted earlier, he is the divine Author of this Book. Its message comes from him. This being so, there is an intrinsic authority in the Bible which no other book has.

Second, for the Christian, the Bible has an authority based upon the lordship of Jesus Christ. When we acknowledge Jesus as our Lord, the Bible's authority over our lives takes on a new dimension. Jesus accepted the Bible as authoritative. His early followers proclaimed its authority and sought to obey its authority as they sought to obey his will. This step in commitment was quite simple for them, as it should be for us. That which was authoritative for our Lord must certainly be authoritative for those of us who follow him.

At the same time, we must be aware that Jesus was very blunt in warning his followers against following the Bible in the same manner which the Pharisees did. For them, the Bible was little more than a legal code, with no need for any thoughtful interpretation at all. Jesus pointed his disciples to the inner principles of the words. It is these for which we must seek.

This brings us right back to the problem of interpreting the Scriptures. Since we do agree that there is an authority in the Bible which is binding upon us and those to whom we minister, we dare not treat its message lightly. We cannot be content with a poor understanding of its message. Therefore, we must not be content with shoddy interpretation. Because the Bible is authoritative, we need to arrive at a clear understanding of what our task as interpreters of the Bible is and how we should go about it.

### The Responsibilities of Interpretation

The very fact that the Bible has an authority which comes from God and that is accepted as authoritative by those who have accepted Jesus as Lord places a significant importance upon our task as interpreters. If a person misinterprets the works of Shakespeare, or those of any other ancient author, his or her life is not affected. The enjoyment of the particular work may be affected, but that is all. But if we misunderstand the authoritative revelation of God, we ourselves are led astray and we may lead others astray who trust us to guide them aright.

This places a heavy responsibility upon the shoulders, hearts, and minds of those who have been called to the task of interpretation. As we seek to interpret the Bible for ourselves and others, we are dealing with life-and-death matters whose ultimate significance will not be known until we move into eternity.

This responsibility of interpretation which rests upon all Christians has two implications. First, there is a personal responsibility to know the truth. A Christian has nothing to fear from truth. No avenue or subject of study which may lead to or shed light upon truth is to be feared. We have the responsibility of seeking to know the truth. There is no excuse for a desire to remain ignorant or for being content with ignorance. The truth of the biblical revelation is never threatened by any truth, anywhere in the world. However, our understanding of the truth of the biblical revelation is severely handicapped by our failure to search for truth. Any truth adds depth to our understanding of the truth of God. Thus, we must bend every effort, tackle any obstacle, and face any foe to come to a personal knowledge of the ultimate truths of God's Word. It is a life-and-death matter for us.

The second implication of the responsibility of interpretation relates to our ministry to others. In whatever way we serve others in the name of Christ, we are involved in interpreting the Scriptures. The involvement may be in witnessing, counseling, teaching, preaching, or in some combination of these. But we, you and I, are involved in interpreting the Bible. Therefore, if we fail to interpret it properly, not only do we fail in guiding people toward God, we will be leading them astray. This responsibility is heavy to bear. Yet it cannot be avoided. The very nature of a commitment to Christ involves interpreting his revelation to others. Fortunately, God's Spirit is both available and active in this ministry. But we dare not allow this to serve as an excuse for poor interpretation. We dare not forget Jesus' scathing denunciation of the scribes and Pharisees at this point (Matt. 23:1-36). They were the most active interpreters of God's word in Jesus' day. But they failed that responsibility, not by avoiding the task, but by doing it wrongly. God forbid that we should fall into this pit.

## The Opportunities of the Interpreter

When we face the responsibilities of the interpreter, there is a certain degree of awe, perhaps even of fear, which overwhelms us. This is as it should be. The responsibility of interpreting the Bible is an awesome one and should be faced in this light. However, this is not the whole story. There is another part of our task which we must consider. This aspect involves the exciting opportunities which God gives through interpreting his Word. Here, too, the opportunities have both personal and corporate dimensions.

Personally, the opportunities of interpreting the Bible involve both our personal spiritual growth and the joy of helping others grow. As we reach better or more complete understandings of the meaning of the Bible, we have the opportunity of growing more according to the pattern which God has planned for us. As we interpret the Bible to others, we experience the excitement of helping them grow into God's pattern. It is not often that anyone has the opportunity of really shaping another's life, both in time and in eternity. The task of interpreting the Scriptures gives us this opportunity.

Corporately, the opportunities which come to us through the avenue of interpreting the Bible are equally as significant. Whether we are thinking of a Sunday School class, a Bible study group, an entire church congregation, or the whole fellowship of believers, our attempts at biblical interpretation affect the growth and maturation of the entire body. Such an opportunity to affect the thought and development of any group of people does not come often.

We need, therefore, to rejoice in these opportunities which God gives to us. But we also need to be prepared to utilize these opportunities when they come. This is a part of our stewardship of the gospel. The servant must be ready to serve when the Master calls.

### Personal Blessings for the Interpreter

Both the responsibilities and the opportunities for interpreting the Bible open doors in the life of the interpreter through which numerous blessings flow. It is a help to keep these before us, especially when the task of mastering the skills of interpretation becomes frustrating and difficult. In listing some of the more significant of these personal blessings for the interpreter, I have not sought to keep them in any particular order of importance. They are all important, and their relative importance varies with time and circumstance.

First, a biblical interpreter is blessed by being allowed to know more about the will and purposes of God. We should never deceive ourselves into thinking we have learned all that there is to know about God. No finite being can every fully comprehend the infinite God. But at least we are allowed to enter into the divine counsel. Any one of us would be excited to get to have this relationship with major national or international leaders. How much more of a blessing it is to have this privilege with God himself.

Second, there is the blessing of knowing that God has considered you worthy of this task. The football player who is given the ball on the last play of the game with three yards to go for a touchdown knows that his team and his coach are trusting him to score. He also knows that they believe he can score. Both of these are sources of encouragement. The same is true of the biblical interpreter. God is trusting you to produce. This trust from God himself is a blessing.

The third blessing for the biblical interpreter comes with the knowledge that, as you interpret the Scriptures to others, you have their lives and destinies in your hands. The trust they give to you in seeking for or listening to your interpretation is significant. This must not be taken lightly.

The fourth blessing which comes to a biblical interpreter who has mastered the skills of interpretation is the knowledge of a job well done. However, it is obvious that unless you do your best, this blessing will not be yours. Doing your best will open the door to the assurance that you have been a good steward of God's revelation, of your own gifts, and of the opportunities and responsibilities which have been set before you.

A fifth blessing for the interpreter of God's Word is that of personal growth. As you become a good biblical interpreter, you should grow spiritually. But you should also find your skills in interpretation improving. The more you do it and the harder you work at it, the better you become. There is no limit to your own growth through this process. God will help you expand your own horizons and abilities as you serve him through this ministry.

## Corporate Blessings from Good Interpretation

Far more important than the personal blessing a good biblical interpreter receives are those received by the group with whom he ministers. Good biblical interpretation aids spiritual growth and enhances the Christian maturing process among those in the group which you serve. A part of this is the developing understanding on the part of the corporate body of how God reveals himself, what he has revealed, and how it is to be applied to life.

One of the common complaints in the early churches was that Christians were staying "babes in Christ," they were not growing up. It is also a common complaint in many churches today. Good biblical interpretation helps us deal with this by aiding the body in its growth. Without good biblical interpretation, a church's theology will be superficial, its emotions childish, and its ministry unbalanced.

Enthusiasm without knowledge to guide it, ignorance which becomes involved in action, and commitments which are founded upon misunderstandings of the Bible are dangerous and may be destructive to the cause of Christ. But good biblical interpretation tackles each of these head-on. Thus blessings come in the form of enthusiastic service guided by spiritual enlightenment, ministry actions carried out by informed servants, and life commitments based upon properly understood biblical foundations.

Fully understood, then, the task of biblical interpretation becomes the source of both opportunity and responsibility for the interpreter. It takes the authority of the Bible seriously, because the interpreter takes the lordship of Jesus Christ seriously. Furthermore, when the interpreter faces the Bible honestly, seeking both to hear the voice of God and to allow that voice to speak to others through the interpreter's words, there result numerous blessings to the interpreter and those around him. The task of the interpreter is both awesome and rewarding. It is well worth the effort required to become a good interpreter of God's biblical revelation.

# 4

# Tools for Interpreting the Bible

No one would wish to go to a surgeon who operated with a rusty knife and a crosscut saw. Neither would we wish to have a dentist who removed teeth with a hammer and a chisel. Furthermore, it would be the height of folly for a forester to try to cut timber with a pair of nail clippers. These suggestions all border on the ridiculous. The foolishness behind them is too obvious to warrant refutation.

It should be just as obvious that the tools needed and used for interpreting the Bible ought to be specifically designed to get the job done. The tragic truth is that many of us who would do none of the foolish things above are often content with tools for interpretation which are just not adequate to accomplish what we are trying to do. The tools we select for aiding us in interpretation are important. If we believe that the biblical message is truly one of life and death, then our tools are as important as the surgeon's tools. If we believe that our message goes beyond time to have an eternal significance, then the quality of our tools becomes even more important.

However, in selecting tools, there are several considerations which we must note. First, it is imperative that the interpreter have the best tools available. Any book store can be found with quantities of cheap books to aid interpretation. But such books are often of poor quality. Relying upon a poor quality tool will produce a poor quality interpretation. I am well aware that books are very expensive and getting more so every day. However, the only thing more costly than good books is not having them. You would not want a surgeon who operated with cheap or outdated equipment. No more should the people to whom we minister have to put up with our use of poor quality, inferior, or outdated equipment for interpretation.

My second word of advice is that you should get tools which you are comfortable in using. This does not mean that the books you obtain should agree with all your ideas. If you are never challenged to consider new thoughts or controversial ideas, your mind and heart will become stagnant, never developing beyond their present capacities. That is a poor stewardship of God's gifts to you. But not every author communicates with every reader. If possible, it is best to check a book out of a library and try it before investing in it. Listen to others' recommendations, but buy the books which communicate well to you. Two photographers, taking the same kinds of pictures, might well use different kinds of cameras and different kinds of film. They use what they are familiar with, what they can trust, and what will give them the results for which they are looking. The same is true for an interpreter. We should not and cannot all be identical in the tools we use.

A third word of advice has to do with the manner in which you use the tools you obtain. Do not become a slave to them. Do not let someone else do your thinking for you. Your tools should be an aid in helping you interpret, not a support upon which you lean to avoid the discipline of interpretation. When you present an interpretation to your people, it is you who are responsible, not your resources. Do not use anyone else's interpretation unless you are willing to answer to God for it. *You will have to answer for your interpretations.* Be sure that you are willing to do so. Interpreting God's Word is a glorious privilege. But it is also a heavy responsibility. Be careful how you do it.

All of this is by way of preamble to our actual consideration of the tools which we need in order to do the job better. Unless we take this advice seriously, we shall not take the selection of our tools of interpretation seriously enough. In the light of these warnings, let us now consider the kinds of tools which are necessary for good interpretation.

## Translations

In approaching the task of interpreting the Bible, we obviously need to know what it says. Therefore, the first tool we need is a text. It should be obvious that the best tools here are the Hebrew Bible for the Old Testament and the Greek New Testament. However, most of us cannot read either Greek or Hebrew. If you have had one or more language courses in seminary training, you probably do not read either one sufficiently well to get by without an English translation. Therefore, we must select a translation or translations from which to work. (This should be done even if you can read Greek and Hebrew.)

Before considering specific translations, we need to consider the very nature of the task of translating. To one unfamiliar with the task, it might appear that it would be simple—merely substituting the best English word for any specific Hebrew or Greek word. In actual practice, it does not work out this way. First of all, there are idioms which cannot be translated literally. Consider for a moment how someone might translate "I like to eat hot dogs for lunch" from English into some other language. The expression, if translated literally, would clearly indicate that we enjoy existing on a diet of heated dog meat! It might be literal, but it would be far from the message intended.

Then there is the problem of one language having words which simply do not exist in another. There is no single English word comparable to the Hebrew word, *hesedh*. It means covenant love, loyal love, steadfastness, mercy, loving-kindness, and commitment. Translating it into simple English terms becomes a major problem for a translator. Further, there is the problem created by the fact that the grammar and syntax of Hebrew and Greek are different from that of English. The Hebrew uses very few adjectives, describing objects in other ways. Consider this example from Isaiah.

> My beloved had a vineyard
> on a very fertile hill (Isa. 5:1*b*).

The Hebrew, having no appropriate adjectives, actually says it this way:

> My beloved had a vineyard
> on a horn, the son of fatness.

The idiom has to be interpreted in order to make any sense to an English reader.

Furthermore, before selecting a translation or translations from which to work, we need to consider and evaluate the various kinds of translations which are available. First, we must clearly differentiate between an actual translation and a paraphrase or amplified translation. There have been a large number of this latter type which have been produced in recent years. One of the more popular, for example, has been *The Living Bible*. Note that amplified translations or paraphrases make no attempt to give a literal translation of the original. Rather, they are an attempt by the author to explain a passage or give its interpretation to its readers. These may be of value for Bible study. They are of little or no value in helping you to become an interpreter, because you have no way of knowing or of even approximating what the original actually said. You have already been made a victim of the interpretation of someone else, with no basis for really making your own interpretation. At the very best, a paraphrase should be given no more significance than a commentary among the tools of the interpreter. More often than not, they are far worse than a commentary, for they offer no reasons for the interpretation which is presented. Thus you have no basis for evaluating it. In no way should a paraphrase ever be used as a tool for trying to determine what a passage originally said.

As far as the Old Testament is concerned, actual translations are usually made by a committee or group of scholars who are seeking to put the ancient text into the best possible English available. By being produced by a group, every word must pass the scrutiny of a number of linguistic specialists who have to be satisfied that the translation is the best possible, given the present state of our knowledge. Yet even these translations fall into two distinct groups.

There are those prepared by scholars from many different religious backgrounds and those which are specifically limited to a particular denominational viewpoint. In addition to these approaches, New Testament translations are frequently prepared by an individual.

Denominational translations may be represented by *The Jerusalem Bible,* a modern language translation specifically prepared by and for Roman Catholics, and the *New World Translation,* prepared by and for the Jehovah's Witnesses. Although an interpreter may use these translations, he needs to be warned that, as might be expected, occasional passages are deliberately slanted toward one or another particular belief. These translations obviously have more value if you are seeking to communicate with persons of those persuasions.

The remaining group translations, made by groups which cut across denominational lines, are those which by their very nature usually approach a more consistent accuracy in presenting the ancient Hebrew or Greek text in English. Perhaps the most common translation is still the King James Version (hereafter KJV). It was originally prepared in 1611, and for beauty of expression is still unexcelled. Its two basic weaknesses both arise from its age. First, much progress has been made in linguistic and textual studies over the intervening centuries. These need to be incorporated into the work of the interpreter. Second, the English language itself has changed over the years. Thus words and expressions which were quite clear when the KJV was prepared are no longer understandable to most modern audiences. The American Standard Version (hereafter ASV) was prepared in the early part of this century. It is one of the more literal translations ever made. But this, in itself, becomes a drawback to its use. Its very literalism frequently makes it sound rather stilted to a modern audience. Also, the same objections raised about the KJV also apply here to a lesser extent. The Revised Standard Version (hereafter RSV) tried to incorporate the best textual and linguistic studies in order to present the biblical text in the clearest modern English, while holding on to as much as possible the beauty of the KJV. An updated version of the ASV has recently been released, called the *New American Standard Bible* (hereafter NASB). Although its aims were the same as the ASV, it is neither as literal as the ASV nor in as smooth English as the RSV. Also recently released has been *The New English Bible* (hereafter NEB). This translation, made by English scholars, was intended to be an updating of the KJV. Unfortunately, it occasionally uses expressions which are unfamiliar to most American readers. It also seems far too frequently to emend a difficult text on the basis of very weak evidence. In addition to these, there have been several other modern translations which the interpreter may wish to use and with which he certainly should at least be familiar.

As noted, translations by individuals are normally confined to the New Testament. The reason for this lies in its comparative brevity and the limited period of history which it covers. Both of these factors make it easier for one person to translate it with greater accuracy and consistency than is possible for the Old Testament. The more familiar of these translations of the New Testament are James Moffatt's *The New Testament: A New Translation*; Edgar Goodspeed's *The New Testament: An American Translation*; and Robert Bratcher's *Good News for Modern Man: The New Testament in Today's English Version*. The value of individual translations is that there is usually a more consistent quality and style throughout. But there is an inherent weakness in that individual idiosyncrasies may creep in with no one to offer corrections.

The interpreter should have several translations available for use in approaching the biblical text. For my purposes, I have used the RSV as the basic text for this book. Any passage not specifically identified will be from the RSV. But in interpretation, however, we confine ourselves to one translation at great risk. If that translation is inaccurate, we have no way of discovering it if that is the only translation which we use. Therefore, throughout this book I shall generally be using at least three translations. The second one which I shall use will be the KJV, due to its very wide circulation. Since most people still use it, at least to some extent, it is wise for the interpreter to include it in his study. Choosing a third translation seems to me to be necessary. If my first two choices should disagree, I need a third to give more information and guidance. Making a choice for a third translation is more difficult, but generally I shall use the NEB or the NASB. Where needed, I will vary this or choose one or more additional versions.

## Dictionaries

The second kind of tools which an interpreter needs is good dictionaries. These fall into several types. First, if you can use Hebrew, then you need a good Hebrew-English lexicon. If you read Greek, you need a good Greek-English lexicon. Without question, the best Hebrew lexicon available for the interpreter is that by Brown, Driver, and Briggs (BDB). There are many others which can be used. There is no other of comparable quality, or which even comes close to it. In the area of Greek, the best lexicon currently available is Walter Bauer, *A Greek-English Lexicon of the New Testament*. Here, too, there are others which are good, but none which seems to be of the same value.

Second, an interpreter needs a good Bible dictionary. These are necessary for looking up difficult biblical terms, getting a quick summary of the history of a city, person, or nation, or otherwise defining a difficult or unclear concept. There are a number of good one-volume Bible dictionaries which the interpreter might use. I personally prefer the *Westminster Dictionary of the Bible*. Insofar as multi-volumed dictionaries are concerned, the *Interpreter's Dictionary of the Bible* is unquestionably the best. Some of you might prefer *Davis Dictionary of the Bible* or *Smith's Bible Dictionary*. In choosing a dictionary, you should find one comprehensive enough to meet your needs but not so technical as to become a hindrance rather than an aid. Generally, the more recent the publication date the better, since biblical studies are constantly evolving.

An interpreter would also be well advised to have a good theological dictionary. For those who know the original languages, the *Theological Dictionary of the New Testament* and the *Theological Dictionary of the Old Testament* (currently in process of publication) are well worth having. For the nonlanguage interpreter, Alan Richardson's *A Theological Word Book of the Bible* is very good and helpful. Such a book will help you trace the development of theological concepts throughout the Bible.

Finally, every interpreter needs a good English dictionary. Since we are interpreting the Bible to other people, we must be able to communicate that interpretation as clearly as possible. It matters not how well you understand a passage; if you cannot explain it clearly, you will have failed. Further, you must also be sure that you properly understand the meaning of the words used in your translation or in your other tools. The best, most up-to-date English dictionary you can afford is an absolute necessity. Words are the basic tools of the interpreter.

## Concordances

Beyond question, other than the Bible itself, the most important tool for the interpreter is a good concordance. This enables the interpreter not only to study a word or passage in its own context but in relation to other Old and New Testament passages. Furthermore, the concordance should be one which is analytical. That is, it should give the word in the original language from which the English word is translated. To this time, there are only three of these which are available. They are Robert Young's *Analytical Concordance to the Bible* (Rev. ed., 1902), James Strong's *Exhaustive Concordance of the Bible* (1894), and the *New American Standard Exhaustive Concordance of the Bible* (1981). The first two are based upon the text of the King James Version. The last is obviously based upon the text of the NASB. There are many other concordances which claim to be complete, but they lack the full analytical value of these. (There is one based only upon the Revised Standard Version of the New Testament, but it is obviously of little value for interpreting the Old Testament.) The reason why an interpreter should have such an analytical concordance appears very quickly when you realize that several different Hebrew or Greek words may be translated by the same English word, while at the same time several different English words may be used to translate one Hebrew or Greek word. Accurate interpretation demands that you know what the original word is which is behind the particular English word or phrase which you are interpreting.

For those who may be unfamiliar with the values of using this kind of concordance, let me point out several of them. First, it will help in determining accurately the meaning of the Hebrew or Greek word which you are considering. An analytical concordance will enable you to consider every passage in the Bible where it occurs. Second, such a concordance will enable you to discover if a word changes in meaning from author to author or from one historical period to another. Since we are dealing with such a long period of time, such changes are to be expected. We need to look out for them. Third, related to the foregoing thought, such a concordance will enable you to trace the historical development of a theological concept throughout the Bible. Fourth, using such a concordance will help you to discover how Old Testament words are carried over into the Greek of the New Testament. This will make it easier for you to carry forward Old Testament roots into their full New Testament flower. Fifth, using this kind of concordance will enable you to do a character study of individuals by looking up every reference to any individual. It will also enable you to do the same kind of study concerning any geographical location by looking up every reference to the place. Sixth, and of least importance, such a concordance will enable you to find a passage when you know any words in it. This is of minor importance here, since the interpreter will usually be starting from an already identified passage, but this may not always be so.

## Histories

Any interpreter of the Bible needs to know as much about the history of the ancient Near East during the biblical period as possible. Since the Bible was written in actual historical settings, recording God's dealings with historical people, the more we know of that history the better off we shall be in our interpretation. Obviously, we cannot know all of the relevant history of these periods and nations. Therefore, it is important to have good historical reference books available. It should go without saying that we should never let these take the place of the Bible itself. Rather, they should be used as tools along with it. At the present time, the best single source for Old Testament history is John Bright's *A History of Israel* (3rd ed., 1981). The best source for the history of the New Testament period is probably Bo Reike's *The New Testament Era*. Obviously, with so much current study going on in the world of the ancient Near East, new historical works are still being produced. It is imperative that the interpreter keep a good, up-to-date reference available.

## Atlases

For the same reason that the interpreter needs a good historical reference, he also needs a good geographical reference. The geography of the biblical world played a significant part in many of its events. To try to understand the Books of Joshua and Judges without good maps before you is sheer folly. To seek to understand the events of David's reign or of Paul's missionary journeys without knowing the general boundaries of the nations involved, or the location of the cities visited, leads to unclear thinking.

It is imperative, then, that the interpreter should have a good historical atlas of the Bible. You not only need to know the general geographical features, the major and minor highways, and the locations of cities, you also need to know how national boundaries changed from period to period. There are several very good historical atlases available. Although it is a bit old, one of the better is still *The Westminster Historical Atlas to the Bible*. Other good ones are *The Bible Atlas* (Broadman) and *The Holman Bible Atlas*. However, the interpreter should get one which is most fulfilling to his own needs. It would be wise to examine several in a library before determining which to buy.

## Archaeology Books

It is obvious that good atlases and good historical works must take into consideration the results of archaeological investigation. At the same time, a valuable tool for you as you approach the Bible is a good survey of the results of archaeological investigation in the lands of the Bible. This may take the form of one volume dealing with the entire Old Testament world or several volumes relating to particular areas, such as Egypt, Palestine, and Mesopotamia.

Not as imperative, but of value if you can afford it, would be a book (or books) which gathers together in English translation the more significant documents from the ancient Near East. Also, a book which has good photographs from the major archaeological sites will be of value. Such a book can show Assyrian and Egyptian reliefs, Roman ruins, and other items of significance, portraying business life, methods of warfare, architectural features, religious items, and relics of daily life which will add understanding to the biblical text. You will have to determine for yourself the relative value of this kind of resource. Certainly, these are of value, but not as much so as most of the other tools of the interpreter.

## Old Testament and New Testament Introductions

You, as an interpreter, need at least one good introduction to the Old Testament and one to the New Testament. This will give you the basic information necessary to understanding the Bible as a whole, as well as giving you specific introductory information to individual books. If possible, you should have more than one of these. Here, too, it is important to get up-to-date books. Biblical scholarship is still developing, so the more recent books will generally be better than the older ones.

A helpful Old Testament introduction is Clyde T. Francisco's *Introducing the Old Testament* (rev. ed., 1977). For a person who is already familiar with the Old Testament, one of the better recent introductions has been that by Brevard Childs. His particular emphasis upon the canon itself as the basic key to interpreting the Old Testament is most helpful and provocative. For the New

Testament, one of the better brief introductions is A. M. Hunter's *Introducing the New Testament.* A more detailed and technical study is the two-volume work by Ralph P. Martin, *New Testament Foundations.* Although not an introduction, a good survey of the message of the New Testament is Frank Stagg's, *New Testament Theology.* A similar survey of the message of the Old Testament is Robert L. Cate's *Old Testament Roots for New Testament Faith.*

The value of an introduction for an interpreter lies in the background which is given for each book, as well as a summary or analysis of its message. No passage should be interpreted until you are familiar with the book in which the passage is found. It is also helpful to know how the passage fits into the developing message of the Bible.

## Commentaries

The final tools which the interpreter needs are commentaries. Commentaries are important for a variety of reasons. They give insight into the background of books. They also give help in the areas of historical, archaeological, geographical, and literary backgrounds to passages. Furthermore, they give aid in studying grammatical and syntactical relations within a particular passage, and assistance in understanding word meanings and developments. Finally, they relate a passage to other similar or significant passages throughout the Bible.

It is important for the interpreter to recognize that there are vast differences both in quality and in the intent of commentaries. There are numerous commentaries which are simply expository in nature. Unfortunately, all they usually offer is predigested interpretation. They do not describe the difficulties or the alternatives for interpretation. They may give you a sermon or a lesson outline quickly, but offer little assistance to you in becoming an interpreter, or in developing skills for interpreting the passage for yourself under the leadership of God. Their chief value will lie in the illustrations they suggest and in offering help in applying a passage after you have interpreted it.

On the other hand, there are good critical, exegetical commentaries which are available. These do not generally offer predigested material. Rather, they gather the available evidence, usually suggest conclusions, but also leave the interpreter free to make his own conclusions. It should be noted that not all commentaries which call themselves critical are actually of that nature. (It should also be noted that a critical commentary is one which gives serious study to a passage, not one which is against it.)

There are at least three types of commentaries which you may use in this part of your tool kit. There is the one-volume kind, which by their very nature are limited. Then, there are those which form a complete set, covering the whole Bible, or at least the Old or the New Testaments. These are made up of many volumes. Finally, there are those commentaries which are not part of a set, but which are written to deal with a particular book or group of books within the Bible. The interpreter could use a single one-volume commentary, at least one full set, and then independent volumes as there is need.

It usually is not wise for you as an interpreter to limit yourself to just one commentary on any particular passage. At least two should be used in order to give a variety of opinions and a better spread of information and background material. It is far better to use three or four. However, you must be aware that the commentators, while scholars in their field, are still only human. You must give proper credence to their skills and abilities, but, at the same time, recognize that they will have a special point of view and may be particularly biased in their interpretations. It will be far more helpful for you to try to make your own interpretation before you begin using your commentaries. In that way, it will be less likely for you to be misled by them.

It would be foolhardy for me to try to suggest the best commentaries. New ones are being produced so often that any suggestions would be quickly outdated. It is far better to suggest that you need thorough, critical commentaries. If you have any ability with Hebrew or Greek, you should have at least one commentary on each book which gives a clear discussion of the original language. In order to help you pick the best commentaries for your needs, visit a good theological library or Christian book store and examine a number of different commentaries. This will enable you to select those which are most helpful for your own needs. Many local churches also have good libraries which you might use.

## Using the Tools

When you, as an interpreter, have gotten the best tools available for your own needs and skills, then you are ready to begin interpreting. It should go without saying that as your own skills and abilities develop, you should add new tools. Further, as we have noted in several places, new discoveries are being made every day which may make some of your good tools outdated. Therefore, keep your tools up-to-date by adding to them constantly. Do not allow yourself to fall into the trap of using the same tools twenty years from now which are adequate for you today. You wish your surgeon to be retraining constantly, utilizing the best tools available at any time. He wants his biblical interpreter to be doing the same.

However, all tools in the world are of no value if you do not use them. Therefore, you must learn how to use them properly.

# Part 2
# Preparing to Interpret
# an Old Testament Text

# 5
# Ensuring a Correct Text

In beginning the task of interpreting any passage in the Old Testament, the very first step must be that of determining what the text really says. Our skills in interpretation will be hampered to a significant degree, if what we are interpreting includes elements that were not part of the original text. This brings us to the study of Old Testament textual criticism.

To some people, however, this concept smacks of blasphemy, or at least infidelity. The very idea that there might be textual variations or scribal glosses appears to undermine the faith of some people. The meaning of these terms and related ones will become clearer as you study this chapter and chapter 7. Scribes often worked in difficult circumstances and had to make decisions while copying a manuscript. Sometimes their decisions resulted in a variation in the text. Do not be afraid of this process for it in no way detracts from the Bible as God's Word. However, we must deal with the fears some people have. In order to do so, let us begin by defining what textual criticism really is.

*Textual criticism is the science of determining as accurately as possible precisely what the inspired author wrote.* In order to develop a technique for doing this, we must first understand how the Old Testament was transmitted. As we begin to understand this, we can then see how variations slipped into the text through the process. Finally, by understanding how variations got into our texts, we shall be in a better position to determine how they might be eliminated.

Before we go further, let me share with you a conclusion which is the result of a lifetime spent in the study of the Old Testament. The study of the text of the Old Testament reveals that there are many scribal glosses which have gotten into it over the years. However, and this is the important part, *there is not a single variation which has yet been discovered which has significantly altered our understanding of any major teaching of the Old Testament.* (The same may also be said of the New Testament.) It almost appears as if God, while leaving copyists free to be human and make mistakes, undergirded the process in such a way as to preserve his message. Now all of this is a very bold assertion. You should not accept it without going through the discipline yourself. However, I believe that when you have gone through the same disciplines and study, you will discover that your experience has confirmed my assertion.

### The Preservation and Transmission of the Old Testament

It is generally assumed by Old Testament scholars that much of the Old Testament was originally passed on in oral form before it was ever recorded in writing. It is obvious, for example, that a sermon by one of the prophets was most likely oral before it was written. Many of the narratives of the patriarchs were probably oral long before they were written. But this is beside the point of our consideration at the moment. What we are concerned with is the written documents. It is our hope to get back to the inspired written material as it was recorded by an inspired writer.

As the ancient Hebrew language developed, it was a part of the Semitic family of languages. In its written form, it was originally written without vowels, without punctuation, and often without spaces between words and sentences. This was probably due to the fact that writing materials were both scarce and relatively expensive. In considering this, we might at first think that it would be unusually difficult to decipher what an ancient text meant. But this is not as difficult as it might seem. To illustrate, consider the word DG. This could either be DIG, DUG, or DOG. Now with this knowledge, the context should make the meaning clear. If a passage spoke of the DG eating a bone or barking, only one choice could fit. If it spoke of a hole in the ground, it would obviously be either DIG or DUG, and further help would be needed. But we are not dealing with isolated words, we are dealing with sentences and paragraphs. As a further illustration, consider the following sentence:

LDMTHRHBBRDWNTTTHCPBRDTGTHRPRDGBN
BTWHNSHGTTHRTHCPBRDWSBRNDSTHPRDGHDNN

It is not difficult to read this as,

Old mother Hubbard
Went to the cupboard
To get her poor dog a bone;
But when she got there,
The cupboard was bare,
And so the poor dog had none.

However, in looking at the original passage, it is quite easy to see how difficult it would be to copy it without a mistake. (In fact, as I wrote it, knowing what I was doing, I made four mistakes in the original.)

It is this which brings us to the basic reason for variations being in the Hebrew text as we have received it. In the ancient world, there were no printing presses. Each copy of any manuscript had to be made by hand. The scribes were copyists. Each time a manuscript was copied, there were numerous opportunities for mistakes to be made, in spite of all the care which went into such a task. Furthermore, once a mistake was in a manuscript, all subsequent scribes copied the mistake which they had been given. In considering this fact, there is no wonder that there are textual variations in the manuscripts as we have them. The real wonder is that there are so few.

To further complicate the task of the student of Old Testament text, there is the fact that, in general. copies were not made until a manuscript was pretty well worn-out. Furthermore, the ancient Hebrews believed that ordinary people should not handle the sacred Scriptures. Thus—rather than risk such sacred texts falling into the hands of someone who was profane—when a new copy was made, the original was usually either burned or buried with the appropriate religious ceremonies. Shortly after a copy was made, the original would be destroyed. This process continued for centuries. This, however, left us without ancient manuscripts with which to compare our copies. Until recently, the oldest complete Old Testament Hebrew manuscript which we had came from about AD 1008. This is obviously more than ten centuries away from the original writing of the latest parts of the Old Testament. (Now we did have copies of the Old Testament in Greek, Latin, and other languages, but these were all translations and are of lesser value in determining the ancient Hebrew text. A translation is never of as much value as a manuscript in the original language.) We did have a few fragments of parts of the Hebrew Old Testament from earlier periods, but no complete books, much less the entire Bible.

It was for this reason that scholars were so excited shortly after World War II by the discovery of the Dead Sea Scrolls. In one fell swoop we were given whole books of the Old Testament, and parts of almost all of it which were centuries older than anything we then possessed. (Part of every book in the Old Testament except Esther has been found among these scrolls.) In studying these ancient Hebrew manuscripts, we found that there were numerous textual variations, just as scholars had suggested all along. The amazing fact was that there was not a single variation of any significance for any major teaching; rather, those variations which had crept into the text were generally insignificant. Those that had gotten there merely illustrated the basic theories of scholars as to how scribal glosses had gotten into the texts in the first place.

The study of these ancient Hebrew manuscripts, coupled with comparison with the ancient versions (translations in other languages), has allowed us to understand with a high level of confidence the transmission of the Old Testament text. We are still a long way removed from the original manuscripts. However, what we have accomplished allows us now to deal with our text with a great deal of assurance of accuracy. We are not on as firm a footing in studying the text of the Old Testament as we are in studying the

New. Nevertheless, we can now approach Old Testament textual studies with solid confidence. We are no longer just dealing with theories but with confirmed theories.

## Categories of Textual Problems in the Old Testament

As noted before, textual variations did get into the Old Testament through the centuries of copying the text from one manuscript to another. In studying these ancient manuscripts, we have been able to identify several specific types of scribal mistakes which can be studied under common categories.

### Accidents in Copying

By far the largest number of textual variations can be classified simply as accidental mistakes. Each of these are easily demonstrable to a person who reads Hebrew, but I shall seek to illustrate them in English.

A common class of accidental textual variations is known as *mistakes of the ear.* These occurred when one person was reading a manuscript to another. The copyist actually wrote a word which sounded like the word pronounced by the reader. For example, if you heard someone read, "The paper was red," you might write it down as, "The paper was read."

The second class of accidental textual variations is *mistakes of the eye.* There are three different types of these. A number of Hebrew letters are similar. The copyists frequently mistook letters for others of similar shape. Furthermore, when identical words or phrases occurred in the same verse or in adjacent verses, the copyist's eyes sometimes skipped from the first to the last, leaving out the intervening words. Additionally, copyists sometimes repeated words or phrases, particularly when they were moving from one line or one column to another.

A less common type of accidental textual variations may be classified as *mistakes of understanding.* This is the third category. As we noted, most ancient manuscripts had neither word nor sentence division. If the scribe was not paying very close attention, when word and sentence divisions were added, these divisions might be made in the wrong places. This seems most often to have happened when the scribe either was not thinking about what he was copying or when he simply did not understand it.

The fourth class of accidental textual variations is known as *mistakes due to confusion*. In many cases, when a scribe copied a manuscript, he caught his own mistakes. However, when he had copied a long scroll, he would not throw it away if there were mistakes in it. Rather, he would try to insert the correct word or phrase in the margin or between the lines. In later years, when someone had to recopy that manuscript, he seldom knew if such additions to the manuscript were actually corrections or were merely scribal notes added for clarification. In such cases, the later scribe had to make his own decision. If he made the wrong one, a variation had gotten into the text. Furthermore, scribes might make explanatory notes in the margin of a manuscript, seeking to clarify difficult passages. In these cases, a later scribe was also faced with the decision as to whether this was a correction or not. If he decided to copy it into the manuscript, we would have an addition which was not really a part of the original text.

### Deliberate Alterations

Although most variations in the Old Testament manuscripts were accidental, there are some intentional alterations. These can generally be demonstrated even to persons who do not read Hebrew.

The most common type of intentional alterations is *changes based upon theology.* Saul had a son by the name of Eshbaal (1 Chron. 8:33; 9:39). The name literally means "man of Baal." But some Old Testament writers thought that it was a shame that any Hebrew leader should be so involved with Baal worship that he would give such a name to his child. Thus, the author of Samuel called this son Ishbosheth (2 Sam. 3:7; 4:1). This name means "man of shame." Here was an intentional change of the text to express a theological comment. Hosea made a similar type of theological comment about the city of Bethel, the major shrine of northern Israel's idolatrous worship. Bethel literally means "House of God." But Hosea constantly referred to it as Beth-aven, which means "House of Iniquity" (Hos. 4:15; 5:8). Other illustrations could be cited.

A second class of intentional alterations is *mistakes of abbreviation.* Very common words or phrases were sometimes abbreviated. But when later scribes came across the abbreviations, they did not always understand these. Consequently, they were frequently treated as mistakes and attempts were made to correct them, leading to textual variations.

The third type of intentional alterations is *scribal mistakes of correction.* When a scribe or copyist was dealing with a passage which was unintelligible, he might try to correct it, using a similar expression from some other place in the Old Testament or by using a more easily understood expression.

Closely related to the mistakes of correction is the fourth category, which I call *variations due to inability to correct.* In such a case, the scribe had a text with an obvious variation. But being aware of his own lack of knowledge and due to his deep respect of the Scriptures, he refused to make any attempt to correct the manuscript, intentionally passing it on with its obvious problem. To illustrate, we are told that "Saul was . . . years old when he began to reign; and he reigned . . . and two years over Israel" (1 Sam. 13:1). Two numbers have been lost from the text over the years. Perhaps a mouse ate a hole in the parchment. But in some way, the numbers were left out. This is obvious. But despite its obvious nature, no scribe ever sought to fill in the gap. (This also serves to illustrate the fact that scribes did handle the Scriptures very carefully.)

In general, this survey of the kinds of textual variations which got into the Old Testament points up two facts. First, the people who copied the ancient manuscripts were human, making the same kinds of scribal mistakes which are made by people who copy written material today. Second, the variations which crept into the

Old Testament text over the years are generally identifiable and correctable. Since this is true, we need briefly to consider the nature of Old Testament textual studies.

## The Nature of Old Testament Textual Studies

In approaching the study of the text of the Old Testament, it is quickly obvious that those who deal with the subject must be highly skilled technicians. At the same time, it is also apparent that, before we can understand how these technicians function, we must first understand something of the nature of the tools with which they work.

### *The Resources Available*

There are a number of kinds of ancient manuscripts which Old Testament textual critics have available. First, there are the Hebrew manuscripts. These include the oldest full manuscript of the Hebrew Old Testament, Codex Leningradensis (so named because it is in a library in Leningrad). This is the standard or authoritative Massoretic Text (MT). It dates from about AD 1008. In addition, there are the massive amounts of materials in the Dead Sea Scrolls, which come from the period between 200 BC and AD 100. Beyond these are several fragments of parts of the Old Testament which come from the centuries between these two extremities.

Second, the textual critics also have available many ancient versions of the Old Testament which have been translated into other languages. Among these are the Septuagint (LXX) in Greek, the Vulgate in Latin, the Peshitta in Syriac, and several others. These are of lesser value than the Hebrew, in spite of their age, due to the fact that they are translations. The very nature of the process of translating one language into another lessens the value of a translation for determining the original. When there is an apparent difference, it may be due to a problem with the Hebrew text. But it may also be due to the translator just trying to make an expression clearer in his own language.

Third, textual critics also use any ancient manuscript or inscription which helps them understand the idioms, figures of speech, grammar, and syntax of the ancient Hebrew. While these are not specifically used to aid in the search for the original text of an ancient manuscript, they add to our knowledge of the language itself. Further, the study of materials in other ancient Semitic languages adds to our understanding of the ancient Hebrew, and thus aids in textual studies.

It can be seen why the textual critic must be such a skilled technician. He must know several ancient languages and be able to read them easily. He must be familiar with a large body of ancient literature, so that he can recognize similarities and differences when he sees them. He must also be familiar with ancient writing and with the changes which both letters and languages underwent over the centuries.

### The Methods

Given these highly technical skills, textual critics have approached the study of the text of the Old Testament. Textual critics are human, and thus are subject to the same weaknesses and prejudices which any other human is likely to have; yet they have generally approached the text of the Old Testament with reverence and respect. In their studies, they have developed a series of techniques by which they approach their task.

1. *Comparison of texts and versions.* Generally, most text critics of the Old Testament begin with the oldest full manuscript of the Old Testament which we have, the Codex Leningradensis. It is compared with all of the older Hebrew books or fragments which we possess. Any and all differences are carefully noted. Then the textual critic compares the passage under study with all of the ancient versions. Here, too, differences are noted. It is this process of comparison which gives the textual critic the list of differences which must be studied. Particular attention is also paid to all difficult passages. When a passage is difficult to translate or to understand, it is also added to the list, even if there are no differences with the ancient texts and versions. Finally, the ancient Massoretes who

preserved the Old Testament Hebrew text for us made lists of difficulties and also recorded ancient translations of textual variations. These, too, must be studied. Therefore, they are also added to the list of passages under study.

2. *Evaluation of problem passages.* Once the list of problem passages has been compiled, the text critic is ready to begin his real work, that of seeking to determine what the original manuscript actually said. Over the years of carrying out these studies, the text critics have developed several basic rules or techniques which guide them in this process. Although most of us will not really be able to become competent text critics, we need to be aware of these so-called rules by which this process is carried out. This will at least enable us to understand what the text critics have done and why different scholars sometimes disagree over some parts of a text.

a. *The rule of meaning.*—Text critics always begin with the assumption that *the biblical author did not write a meaningless text.* No one who has a message to communicate is going to write nonsense. Further, God certainly did not inspire a meaningless text. The basic thrust of the Bible is that God sought to communicate his truth to mankind. He always did it in terms which men could have understood. Therefore, the text critic assumes that the text must have meaning.

However, experience has taught us that just because we do not understand the meaning of a text does not mean that it is not understandable. Our knowledge of ancient languages and customs is still quite limited. Discoveries are constantly being made which enable us to understand passages which formerly had appeared to be nonsensical. Therefore, lack of meaning does not necessarily mean that a passage has a textual problem in it. It may just be an indication of our own ignorance. Text critics do assume that any text should have meaning, and they seek to determine that meaning.

b. *The rule of difficulty.*—In general, text critics approach the analysis of a text from the standpoint that *the most difficult text is probably the correct one.* It is far more likely that ancient scribes would have tried to simplify a text than that they would have made it more difficult. Thus, in comparing ancient manuscripts, difficulty is considered to be a likely criterion for originality.

c. *The rule of explanation.*—Equally important to text critics is the assumption that *the passage which most naturally explains the origin of the others is most likely to be the original.* When there are several variations to a particular verse, it is far more likely that the one which most easily and logically fits at the beginning of a developmental process is the correct one.

d. *The rule of antiquity.*—Text critics also use the assumption that *the text which is the oldest is most likely the correct one.* However, this rule must be applied with a great deal of care. The antiquity of a text does not necessarily prove anything. An ancient text could have a scribal gloss while a more recent one could represent a more accurate copy of the original.

By using these four rules and applying them with the skills developed over a lifetime of study, the Old Testament text critic begins moving toward the original manuscript which was written. It should be noted that many of the conclusions which text critics had reached concerning the Old Testament text by using these rules were confirmed by the discovery of the Dead Sea Scrolls. Thus, we were at least assured that our approach was valid. We must note, however, that Old Testament textual studies are not yet as assured as New Testament textual studies are. Due to the comparative scarcity of ancient Hebrew manuscripts, we cannot say that we can be certain of every verse in the Old Testament. But we are steadily moving in the direction of such assurance.

In the approach which most of us must make to the Old Testament, we are in the hands of the text critics. We must trust them, for we do not have the skills to do the work ourselves. However, the results are well enough attested that we can approach the results of their work with assurance. We can begin our task of interpretation by assuming that the work of the text critics has provided the translators with an Old Testament text in which we can have confidence.

## Arriving at a Tentative Translation

In seeking to begin the process of interpretation of any Old Testament passage, you and I generally begin with the English text. However, there are a number of steps through which we must go in order to arrive at the specific text which we shall actually be using in our interpretation. You will need to choose at least three translations from which to work. As I indicated in chapter 4, "Tools for Interpreting the Bible," I shall use the RSV and KJV in this book. With these, I will usually use the NASB or the NEB (sometimes both). You should use those translations which you find best suited for the task. However, I strongly urge that you do begin with the KJV and the RSV.

Step 1. *Arrange the biblical material in a manner which will most easily facilitate comparison.* Normally, this would involve writing the verse from the various translations either in parallel lines or in parallel columns. I prefer parallel lines, but you should try both and then decide which is better for you. If you can read the Hebrew, it should always be the first line or the first column. This should be followed by your own translation. Then, you should use at least three different translations in your comparison. Four would be better. (Also, note any variant translations suggested by marginal notes.)

Step 2. Go through the various translations in your arrangement and *underline those words or expressions which differ significantly from one another.* Normally, I use a different colored pen for each difference. In the examples which follow, these differences will be indicated with bold type. You should ignore differences which are simply Old English expressions, such as "hath" and "has." Also, at this point, you should ignore differences in punctuation unless they significantly change the meaning.

Step 3. Seriously *consider the differences in the various translations.* Question whether there are real differences or merely that the translator is substituting words which are synonymous. At this point, you should refer both to a Bible dictionary and an English dictionary. Also, you should consult at least two commentaries to discover what insights they might shed on translation difficulties and word meanings.

Step 4. When all of this has been done, you are in a position to *make a tentative translation of the verse for yourself.* As you do so, keep in mind the audience for whom you are making the translation. You would certainly use different words for a group of six-year olds than you would for a group of college young people. Do not decide on words or phrases just because they happen to agree with your preconceived ideas or theology. Remember God's words to Job,

> Who is this that darkens counsel
>     by words without knowledge? (Job 38:1).

You should also remember God's condemnation of Job's friends, when he said to Eliphaz, "My wrath is kindled against you and against your two friends; for you have not spoken of me what is right" (42:7). These should warn us of the danger of seeking to make the Bible say what we want instead of listening to what it really says.

Step 5. *Keep reminding yourself that your translation is only tentative.* As you continue through the entire task of interpretation, you may discover that you need to modify or correct your translation. No translation should be final until you have completed the entire task of interpretation. Your interpretation can never ultimately be better than your translation. It is our task not to say what the Bible should have said or might have said, but to know what it did say and then to understand it and to apply it to the lives of ourselves and the people to whom we minister.

If all of this sounds like hard work, it is. But if, as we claim to believe, we are dealing with the very words of life, with the very word of God, then we dare not be content with anything less than our very best. We will discover that as we use this process, it will become somewhat easier. *But it will never be easy.* You may discover many precious treasures in the Old Testament by methods far less rigorous than this. But without some similar method, you will never even begin to come close to the full riches of the treasures of God's word in the Old Testament.

## Selected Examples

It is easier to see how to apply the foregoing steps by noting some specific examples. In setting up these, I have chosen both prose and poetry, both narrative and sermonic materials. Go through these carefully. To make it more typical, I have neither put in the Hebrew nor my own translation. Numbers in parentheses are guides to the discussions of the differences in the translations.

1. Genesis 2:7

KJV:   And the Lord God formed **man** (1)
RSV:   Then the Lord God formed **man**
NEB:   Then the Lord God formed **a man**
NASB:  Then the Lord God formed **man**

KJV:   **of the** dust **of** the ground (2,3)
RSV:   **of** dust **from** the ground,
NEB:   **from the** dust **of** the ground
NASB:  **of** dust **from** the ground,

KJV:   and breathed into his nostrils the breath of life;
RSV:   and breathed into his nostrils the breath of life;
NEB:   and breathed into his nostrils the breath of life.
NASB:  and breathed into his nostrils the breath of life;

KJV:   **and** man became **a living soul.** (5)
RSV:   **and** man became **a living being.**
NEB:   **Thus** (4) man became **a living creature.**
NASB:  **and** man became **a living being.**

(1) **A man** or **man**? The majority would go with **man**, but that is not the best way of making such a decision. The commentaries which discuss it point out that the Hebrew expression used here either refers to a specific, individual man or to mankind in general. It appears that the context is referring to the general creation of man in this passage in the same way that it later refers to the general creation of animals. However, the Genesis account quickly moves to

the consideration of a specific individual. But it does not in any way refer to just any man. Thus it would seem wise to reject *a man* from our translation, using simply *man*.

(2) The preposition used with *dust* appears to be immaterial. However, there is no reference to any specific *dust*, so the definite article probably should be rejected from before *dust*.

(3) Whether you use *from* or *of* with "the ground" depends upon the shades of meaning which each implies to you. The passage was clearly indicating the source of "the dust" from which man was made. It appears to me that *from* is the preferable word.

(4) The choice in the final phrase between *and* or *thus* again depends upon the shade of meaning which each implies to you. What happened to man was the direct result of the act of God, a specific consequence. *Thus* appears to me better to carry the force intended.

(5) There have been a lot of sermons preached upon the fact that the difference between man and the animals is that man was made *a living soul*. Unfortunately, old sermons can frequently color our translation and our interpretation. It ought to be the other way around. However you translate this phrase, you must note that the identical expression was used to describe the animals in Genesis 1:20-21. Since there is nowhere in the Bible a concept that animals have souls, then we must turn to our other possibilities, *living being* or *living creature*. Actually, there is really very little difference between these two expressions. However, although man was clearly created by God, the particular expression used here apparently makes no reference to his creation. Rather, the emphasis of this phrase points simply to the fact that man was living, existing. Thus, I would prefer *living being*.

*Tentative Translation:* And the Lord God formed man of dust from the ground, and breathed into his nostrils the breath of life; thus man became a living being.

2. Isaiah 45:22-23

    KJV:    *Look* unto *me,* and be ye saved, (1)

RSV:     *Turn* to *me* and be saved,
NEB:     *Look* to *me* and be saved,
NASB:    *Turn* to *Me,* and be saved, (2)

KJV:     *all the ends* of the earth:
RSV:     *all the ends* of the earth! (4)
NEB:     *you peoples from all corners* (3) of the earth;
NASB:    *all the ends* of the earth;

KJV:     for I am God, *and there* is *none other.*
RSV:     For I am God, *there* is *no other.*
NEB:     for I am God, *there* is *no other.*
NASB:    For I am God, *and there* is *no other.* (5)

KJV:     I have sworn *by myself,*
RSV:     *By myself* I have sworn, (7)
NEB:     *By my life* (6) I have sworn,
NASB:    I have sworn *by Myself,* (2)

KJV:     *the word is gone out of my mouth in righteousness,*
RSV:     *from my mouth has gone forth in righteousness* (8)
NEB:     *I have given a promise of victory,* (8)
NASB:    *The word has gone forth from My mouth in righteousness* (2)

KJV:     and *shall not return,* (9)
RSV:     *a word* that *shall not return:*
NEB:     *a promise* that *will not be broken,*
NASB:    And *will not turn back,*

KJV:     That unto me every knee *shall bow,* (10)
RSV:     'To me every knee *shall bow,*
NEB:     that to me every knee *shall bend*
NASB:    That to Me every knee *will bow,* (2)

KJV:     every tongue *shall swear.*
RSV:     every tongue *shall swear.'*
NEB:     *and by me* (11) every tongue *shall swear.*
NASB:    every tongue *will swear allegiance.* (12)

(1) *Turn* or *look*? Neither word is a precise translation of the

Hebrew expression used here which literally means "turn your face." Obviously, you cannot do this without turning. However, you must judge as to whether or not the context implies that God expected more than a simple redirection of life. Was he also expecting men to look at him, to follow him? I think so, but it becomes a matter of personal interpretation. Either word is acceptable. *Turn* is the bare minimum, but *look* appears to be preferable from my standpoint.

(2) The next problem shows up in at least four places in these verses, and that concerns the capitalization of pronouns referring to God. Various translations adopt different styles. Of the four I am using, only the NASB capitalizes such pronouns. The reason the others do not is that there are no capitals in Hebrew at all. Therefore, making a pronoun refer to God is always a matter of interpretation. Some places clearly refer to God, others do not. Many are unclear. When a translation capitalizes any pronouns, then it automatically implies that all places where they are not capitalized clearly do not refer to God. On the other hand, when none are capitalized, then the interpreter clearly knows that he must make the decision every time he comes across a pronoun. It therefore appears to me to be better to leave them all not capitalized, forcing the interpreter to think for himself rather than depending upon the decisions of the translators.

(3) *You peoples from all corners* is clearly an interpretation of *all the ends*, and is therefore to be rejected as a translation. It is obviously people who are expected to turn, but that is still an interpretation and not a translation.

(4) The exclamation point following "earth" is clearly an interpretation in the RSV and probably should be rejected. However, the verb "look" is a command, and the punctuation might be justifiable from that point of view.

(5) The difference between *and there* and *there* is insignificant. The same is true of *none else* and *no other*.

(6) *By my life* is an interpretation of the more basic *by myself*. As a translation, the latter is far preferable. God does not just swear

by his life, but by his very nature, by his whole being and character.

(7) The word order of this phrase in the RSV and the NEB differs from the other two, but is the correct form. The commentaries point out that the position of *by myself* in the Hebrew sentence is emphatic. Therefore the translation should show this emphasis. To me, "By myself I have sworn" is far more emphatic than the simple statement, "I have sworn by myself."

(8) *I have given a promise of victory* is quite interpretive and is to be rejected for a translation. It would also appear that the RSV has probably misplaced *a word* at this point.

(9) Again, the NEB appears to be interpreting rather than translating with *will not be broken*. On the other hand, there is only a slight difference between *shall not return* and *will not turn back*. The latter expression appears to me to be a bit stronger and I accept it for that reason. But I am well aware that there is not much difference either way.

(10) We are so familiar with the expression, "every knee shall bow" within the Christian community that it may strike us as strange to realize that this is not a common thought outside of Christian churches. People normally speak of bending the knee and bowing the head. Thus it appears that *shall bend* really is a more communicative English expression.

(11) *And by me* of the NEB is not in the Hebrew. It is certainly implied by the preceding phrase, "to me every knee shall bend," but a good translation leaves the implications up to the interpreter and does not add them to the translation.

(12) The expression *swear allegiance* of the NASB is interpretive rather than a translation. The commentaries point out that this is the same verb root used for God's swearing in the preceding verse. He certainly was not swearing allegiance. Thus this is to be rejected here. It is probably a good interpretation, but a poor translation.

(13) It should also be noted that all of the translations except the KJV clearly indicate that this passage is poetry. Thus, our tentative translation should reflect this by its form, alerting us to the fact as we later approach the interpretation.

*Tentative Translation:*

> Look unto me, and be saved,
>> all the ends of the earth;
>> for I am God, and there is no other.
> By myself I have sworn,
>> the word has gone forth from my mouth in righteousness
>> and will not turn back,
> that to me every knee shall bend,
>> every tongue shall swear.

## Practice Exercises

It would be simple for me to keep on multiplying examples of this process. For me to do so would be to deny you the right of developing your own skills and abilities. But before you select just any passage and try to do it, I want to suggest two passages which will enable you to begin practicing. If you will do these as I have done the first two, you will find real help by dealing with the questions which I have outlined.

1. Genesis 12:3

(1) Write the verse from several different translations as it was done in the two examples.

(2) Particularly note the variant translations suggested by the RSV and by the NASB.

(3) The major problem to be considered is the last phrase. Does it say that the "families of the earth shall bless themselves" or that the "families of the earth shall be blessed"? You will need to check at least two good commentaries in order to answer this.

2. Jeremiah 2:10-13

(1) Write the verse as done in the examples.

(2) Note the differences in the geographical references. Which should be used?

(3) Carefully consider the emotions which the heavens are asked to exhibit. Which ones appear to be the best choices for a translation?

(4) What variant translations are suggested for "fountain"? Do any of these communicate better than "fountain"? Why do you think so?

(5) Is there a better expression used than "broken cisterns"? What is it? Why do you think it is better?

## 3. Other Suggestions

Now, before you begin selecting passages at random upon which to work, let me suggest that you try a few others without the guidance of my questions. Try Jeremiah 17:9-10; Amos 3:3-8; 5:21-24; and Micah 7:18. Each of these gives particular problems with which you will have to grapple as you begin to build up your skills.

When you start making random selections, you might try several narrative passages first. These usually are not as difficult as those in the Psalms or in the sermons of the prophets. Let me warn you again, do not expect it to be easy. However, if you persist in your practice, you will find that your skills and your confidence will develop. Remember, the better tools you have at this point, the better your results will be. However, tools can never replace personal skill. They merely enhance it.

## Sample Work Sheet

### ARRIVING AT A TENTATIVE TRANSLATION

Text: Book, chapter, and verses
1. Arrange the text in parallel lines. Underline significant differences.

2. Evaluate the differences. List reasons for your decisions.

3. Tentative Translation. (Let your form show prose or poetry.)

# 6

# Determining What the Text Says

It is essential to be as sure as possible that you have an accurate translation to interpret. No interpretation can possibly be any better than the translation which you are interpreting. However, when you have arrived at a tentative translation, you are really just ready to begin the actual labor of interpretation. To this point, all that you really have is just a collection of words. Now comes the next step, that of determining what the text really says.

In beginning to work on this, you must be aware of several warnings. First, determining what an Old Testament text really says is not normally as difficult as doing the same thing with a New Testament text. Sentences in the New Testament are usually much longer, much more involved, and, therefore, much more difficult to grasp all at one time. But do not let this lull you into carelessness or overconfidence. This is still a step which must be carefully mastered and to which you must constantly give serious thought.

Second, determining what an Old Testament text says is not as subjective as some have suggested. It has been said that you can make a text mean just about what you want it to mean. As an illustration, it has been suggested that the process is somewhat similar to interpreting the sentence, "Time flies like an arrow." The normal interpretation of this is that time passes through our lives with unhindered speed. But, suppose that "flies" is a noun and that the verb of this sentence is "like." Then our sentence talks about "time flies" (possibly related to "houseflies" and "horseflies") which are attracted to an arrow. (Perhaps they like to cuddle up to it at night.) But then along comes another interpreter who claims that the verb is "time," which is a command to take out a stopwatch and time those little flies as they zoom by.[1]

Now it is obvious that if this kind of freedom is allowed to an interpreter, then we can certainly make a passage mean just about whatever we want it to mean. However, there are at least two fallacies in this approach. The first is that any text which you are interpreting is located in a context. What is in the verses immediately before and after your text clearly gives you boundaries for determining what a text says. Further, while in the English it is impossible to know if the verb in our illustration is "time," "flies," or "like," that is not true in the Hebrew. There, the various parts of speech are usually clearly identifiable. Thus, we can make a passage mean what we want it to only by ignoring both the grammatical forms and the syntactical arrangement of the sentence and by ignoring its context. No serious interpreter would do either.

Third, in determining what a text says, you will need to develop all your skills in the language arts. You should become a master of grammar and syntax, as well as word meaning and word usage. Furthermore, you will need to do this not only in English, but, for the Old Testament, you will need at least to become familiar with basic principles of these concerns in the Hebrew language. Whether or not you read Hebrew, there are some basic facets of the language with which you must be familiar if you are going to achieve satisfactory results at this point. The words of a text were put together by the inspired writer to communicate God's truth. His word had a specific arrangement and a message to communicate. Thus, we must begin to look for the sense of the words in our text.

It is obvious that God can and does use us in spite of our failings. But we must seek to give him our very best at this point also. Anything less is poor stewardship of his revelation. Mastering the language arts will bring an added benefit to you as an interpreter. Not only will you be able to understand what a text says, you also will be better able to share that understanding with others. There is no excuse for poor communication of the gospel from those of us who have been given this task. We must remind ourselves that it is "by the foolishness of preaching" (KJV) that God saves, not by foolish preaching (see 1 Cor. 1:21).

## Consider the Grammar

Before you consider the grammar of your English translation, there are some basic points of Hebrew grammar with which you must become familiar. First, we must understand the concept of verb tense. The word *tense* as related to a verb concerns the time in which the action occurred. Thus, in English we speak of verbs in the present tense (action in the present time), verbs in the past tense (action in past time), and verbs in the future tense (action in the future). *Hebrew does not have tenses.* Hebrew verbs do not indicate the time of an action. Rather, they indicate the "state" of the action. Thus a Hebrew verb may be classified as being in the "imperfect state," with the action viewed as not completed, or in the "perfect state," with the action viewed as completed.

Now to us, it would appear that incomplete action must be in the present or future time, while completed action must be in the past. This was not the way the ancient Hebrews saw it. They could speak of a future action as completed, if they were viewing it from that position. Further, they could also look at past action as incomplete, if they viewed it from a past standpoint. In addition, they could describe a future action as being completed, based upon the authority of God. (This is what is known as a "prophetic perfect.") To the ancient Hebrew, the time of the action of a verb was always determined from the context, and not from the verb itself. Thus, "to us a child is born," (Isa. 9:6) can just as well be translated (from the grammatical form) as "to us a child has been born" or "to us a child shall be born." What the translator sees in the context will determine which of these clauses he will choose. It is imperative that you remember the difference between Hebrew verb states (complete or incomplete) and the actual time of action a verb describes.

The second major point of Hebrew grammar with which you should be familiar is that Hebrew sentences are generally short and uninvolved. Their language did not lend itself well to complex sentences. They preferred short clauses and usually did not get involved with long, complex sentence structures.

Further, there are very few adjectives and adverbs in Hebrew. Thus, most Old Testament statements are short and to the point. It was a good language for describing action or communicating what God expected of his people. It was not a language which lent itself well to philosophical thought or to theological reflection. Thus the Old Testament makes very few theological statements about God. On the other hand, the Old Testament is clear concerning God's actions in history.

Now in relating this to your personal translation, you need to keep these facts in mind. Seek to identify the verbs in your translation. Are they describing completed action or incomplete action? You should also question whether or not the time given to the action in your translation is correct. Does the context really show why the translator placed the verb in past, present, or future time? Does it appear that the text should be placed in a different time from that used by the translators? These are questions with which you must grapple and which you must answer. In beginning, you will feel quite unsure and incompetent. But you will build up skills as you persist. Obviously, you will be better able to deal with these if you can use Hebrew yourself. But with the use of your own God-given sense, the leadership of his Spirit, and the use of good commentaries, you can arrive at adequate answers without knowing Hebrew.

Furthermore, if your own translation begins to have an involved sentence structure, you can rest assured that you are getting away from what the author was saying. Do not let too many adjectives or adverbs creep into your translation. The Old Testament text is generally simple. If you would really know what a text says, you should strive to keep your translation simple.

## Consider the Syntax

Syntax is the study of word relationships within a sentence or clause. In understanding what an Old Testament verse really says, syntax is of paramount importance. Unfortunately, in trying to make a smooth English sentence from a Hebrew sentence, a translator virtually destroys most evidence of what the Hebrew syntax was.

To illustrate this, consider the fact that the normal word order of a Hebrew sentence is the verb (and its modifiers), followed by the subject (and its modifiers), followed by the direct object (and its modifiers), followed by the indirect object (and its modifiers). But to try to translate that into English in an exactly parallel word order would make no sense. Therefore, all the translator can do is try to put a normal Hebrew sentence into a normal English sentence. Any variation in the Hebrew word order is for emphasis. Therefore, if something is emphasized in the Hebrew, the translator must try to make some modification in the normal English sentence to emphasize that same part of the text. However, the techniques of indicating emphasis in an English sentence are not as simple or as straightforward as they are in Hebrew. Thus, different translators use different devices to try to point out what the biblical author was emphasizing.

However, all of this leaves you as the interpreter somewhat at a loss in determining where the emphasis of the text actually lies. But it is not an irretrievable loss. First, you should read your translation (which has been based on a careful analysis of several translations) thoughtfully, seeking to determine what the English sentence appears to emphasize. Good translators can make their translation emphasize the same things as the Hebrew. Your tentative translation should reflect these emphases. Note where the English word order is different from what you would have normally expected. A variation in word order is the most common device for indicating emphasis.

After you have tried to identify the emphasis for yourself, refer to your commentaries. Note where they place the emphasis. By checking and cross-checking, you should be able to decide with reasonable assurance where the emphasis is.

It is worth noting that there is no special emphasis made in most verses of the Old Testament. Do not try to manufacture an emphasis when the statement is straightforward. However, you do need to be able to recognize a syntactical emphasis when you see it. Consider the two tentative translations we developed in the preceding chapter.

> And the Lord God formed man of dust from the ground, and breathed into his nostrils the breath of life; thus man became a living being (Gen. 2:7).

> Look unto me, and be saved,
>   all the ends of the earth;
>   for I am God, and there is no other.
> By myself I have sworn,
>   the word has gone forth from my mouth in righteousness
>   and will not turn back,
> that to me every knee shall bend,
>   every tongue shall swear (Isa. 45:22-23).

In reading the first text, nothing really stands out on the basis of word order. There does not appear to be any special syntactical emphasis. If that is your conclusion, you are correct. There is no special emphasis in the Hebrew. The Isaiah passage, however, is a bit different. The normal way of beginning the second verse would be, "I have sworn by myself." But the order has been changed in the English. It would appear that the expression "by myself" is being emphasized. Again, if that is your conclusion, you are correct. The Hebrew word order places a significant emphasis upon this expression.

A second feature also stands out from the study of Hebrew syntax. The very fact that the verb is normally placed first in a sentence should alert you to the fact that the Hebrews placed a major emphasis upon action. This is why the Old Testament stories are so readable and so entertaining. A typical child is much more enthralled by the stories about Abraham, Moses, David, and Daniel than he is by the writings of Paul. It is the action which gets and keeps his attention. For the adult who approaches the Old Testament, it is still the action which captures his imagination. But adults are not only captivated by the acts of men. We are generally also captivated by the mighty acts of God. This is why the Old Testament has been called the book of the acts of God. It does not set forth great statements about God nearly as often as it describes the deeds of God. Israel learned of God's character by seeing his acts. They bore witness to his character by telling of his acts. Thus, in coming to grips with what any text in the Old Testament says, you should pay careful attention to the verbs, to the action.

## Consider the Punctuation

The next step in determining what an Old Testament text really says is made by carefully noticing the punctuation. As we have noted, the original manuscripts of the Old Testament did not have any punctuation in them. But when Hebrew became a dead language, the Massoretes developed a system of accents which sought to record for future generations precisely the manner in which those ancient manuscripts had been read. It is from these ancient accents that most modern translators get their basic system of punctuation. Admittedly, these accents may not be as authoritative as the text itself, but they certainly preserve the oldest traditions we have as to how a text was read and understood.

The punctuation indicates how the verse was divided into phrases. Clauses and phrases are separated by commas, major breaks are indicated by colons and semicolons. Sentences are separated by periods, exclamation points, and question marks. These should all be carefully noted. In determining what the verse really says, you cannot ignore these punctuation marks. On the other hand, you should be aware that translators and commentators will disagree with one another regarding how a verse should be punctuated. Generally, when one makes a significant divergence from the normal punctuation, he will offer an explanation. Then you must consider that explanation and make your own decision. Let me warn you, never accept a major change in punctuation just because it sounds good. Unless a translator or commentator gives sufficient evidence for making his change, I would strongly urge that you do not ignore the ancient tradition of the Hebrew accents.

In Isaiah 9:6, the names of the Messiah are given by the translators in two different ways. The KJV lists them as "Wonderful,

Counsellor, The mighty God, The everlasting Father, The Prince of Peace." The RSV, on the other hand, makes the five names into four, calling him: "Wonderful Counselor, Mighty God, Everlasting Father, Prince of Peace." The commentaries point out that since the last three names are all double names, the first one should be as well. However, they are quick to note that the accentuation in the Hebrew does divide the first name. At this point, you have to make your own decision. Are you going to stick with the accentuation, or are you going to go with the parallel construction? (Personally, I still go along with the accentuation, seeing five names instead of four.)

It should be noted that this kind of problem does not develop very often. The Hebrew accents usually give good sense to the inter-pretation of a verse. If you are going to have a clear idea of what the text says, you must pay close attention to the punctuation which reflects these accents.

## Consider Word Usages

Once you have the grammar, syntax, and punctuation clear in your mind, you are well on the way to determining what your text says. The next step is to consider word usages. By that, I mean that you must come to a clear understanding of how the Old Testament actually used the words in the text you are interpreting. This involves three different aspects of investigation: individual words, idioms, and figures of speech.

In investigating how the Hebrews used individual words, an analytical concordance becomes your primary tool. It is imperative to see the variety of ways a specific word is translated as well as the various contexts in which it is used. A good commentary dealing with your specific text may help here, but it can never replace a thorough study of the references given by your analytical concor-dance. Consider, for example, the concluding phrase in Micah 7:18: "he delights in steadfast love." The KJV translates this as, "he delighteth in mercy," which seems to be quite different. By referring to the concordance, we discover that "mercy" translates the Hebrew word *hesed*. In going through its other usages, we discover that the word refers to the loyal love which God bestows upon his people. If you are very thorough in looking up all of the passages where it is used, you will discover that it seems generally to refer to the love which God promised and gave through his covenant to Israel. It can be translated as "mercy," "steadfast love," and "loyal love," and thus appears to include more than any of the words used. It is actually a key word for understanding both the Old Testament awareness of God's loyalty to his promises and its grasp of his very nature.

Another example of the process for determining the Hebrew usage of words can be seen in the word *judge* as seen in Judges 2:16-19 and other places. Your analytical concordance shows that this word is a translation of the Hebrew word *shaphat*. In examining the various places where this word is used, we discover that it in no way is limited to our concept of a judge as one who presides over a courtroom. Instead, the word appears to refer to one who is specially gifted, empowered by God, and raised up as a political, military, and occasionally as a religious leader.

We have already called your attention to the usage of the word *perfect* in describing both Noah and Job (Gen. 6:9; Job 1:8; 2:3; see "The Languages of the Bible," in ch. 2). There the Hebrew word *tamin* refers to maturity rather than to moral perfection. This word thus describes Job and Noah as being mature in their relationships with God and man. A determination of their moral character must be made elsewhere.

A second area of word investigation which must be carried out is that of identifying and becoming familiar with Hebrew idioms. An idiom is a common expression which has developed a meaning that would in no way be apparent from a literal rendering of the words involved. Varying an earlier illustration, consider the foreigner who was taken to his first baseball game. When his host ordered two hot dogs, he was horrified, for he had no desire to eat dog meat! To a foreigner, unfamiliar with American idioms, there is no way by which he could ever guess that a hot dog was a spicy sausage. The same is true of any language, including biblical Hebrew. There are idioms which developed which have a meaning that appears to be quite unrelated to the literal meaning of the words used in the expression. In general, good translators will have already taken care of this for you, but not always. If you are doing your own translation, you must be especially careful with idioms. A certain degree of care must be exercised at all times. Consider Psalm 19:7-9.

> The law of the Lord is perfect,
>   reviving the soul;
> the testimony of the Lord is sure,
>   making wise the simple;
> the precepts of the Lord are right,
>   rejoicing the heart;
> the commandment of the Lord is pure,
>   enlightening the eyes;
> the fear of the Lord is clean,
>   enduring forever;
> the ordinances of the Lord are true,
>   and righteous altogether.

The "fear of the Lord" stands out like a sore thumb right in the middle of five other expressions referring to some form of law or commandments. Could it be that this is an idiom for the authoritative, revealed laws of God? In following the usage of this expression as listed by your analytical concordance, you will find numerous references which would seem to confirm this. Moses called the Ten Commandments, "the fear of him" (Ex. 20:20). Isaiah condemned his people for turning away from God, for God had said, "Their fear of me is a commandment of men" (Isa. 29:13). Thus, it begins to appear that "the fear of the Lord" ( or "me," or "him") was an idiom which referred to God's authoritative demands upon his people.

A third area of investigation which needs to be carried out in regard to word usage involves figures of speech. Every language has a variety of figures of speech which must be interpreted in order to understand what a passage is really saying. Thus, the serpent in Genesis 3 is certainly a figure of speech for Satan. If you take the serpent literally, all you have there is a story of why people and snakes do not get along together, with a promise that mankind will ultimately defeat "serpentkind." Obviously, this is far from what the Genesis writer was saying. Note also, the statement in Isaiah 44:22:

> I have swept away your transgressions like a cloud,
>     and your sins like mist;
> return to me, for I have redeemed you.

There are three figures of speech here. The first is that of God sweeping. In no way are we to view God as starting out with a broom to sweep away sins. But the image is that of a thorough cleansing, as if he had used a broom. Further, transgressions are not cloud, neither are sins mist. The whole message of the Bible would scream out against this. But when God starts dealing with something as solid and heavy as our transgressions and our sins, they become like a cloud and mist. He removes them from us that thoroughly.

So in determining what the ancient writers were saying, it is imperative that we investigate the usage of words. We must identify word meanings, idioms, and figures of speech. But there are still other steps in determining what the text says.

## Consider Contemporary Word Meanings

The next step in this particular process involves our knowledge of contemporary word meanings. To a large extent, this also involves knowing the way the people to whom we minister use words. We can put our tentative translation in the best, clearest biblical and theological language, and no one may understand us. Most people who have grown up in a Christian church may have a fairly good awareness of what grace is. But to the average person on the street, the word will convey little or no meaning. There is a delightful book title calling attention to this particular problem, *Grace Is Not a Blue-Eyed Blonde* (by R. Lofton Hudson). It is imperative that we put our resultant translation into words which communicate precisely what we understand the text to say.

At this point, you will bring your English dictionary into use, as well as your knowledge of people. Carefully consider every word in your translation. Look up any words of whose meaning you are in the least unsure. Consider the audience to whom you are going to eventually present your interpretation. Will they understand what you mean by the words you have chosen? Will they understand the idioms, or the figures of speech?

There are two key concepts which you need to practice at this point—*clarify* and *simplify*. The words you select should be stepping-stones to understanding, not stumbling blocks. If you were interpreting Genesis 6:9, it would be unwise to use the word *perfect* for most church congregations or Sunday School classes. It would not be expected that they would properly understand the biblical emphasis. Or, if you do use the word, be sure that you make a time to explain the meaning of the word. On the other hand, it will be next to impossible to come up with one word or expression which will carry the full meaning of *hesed* as found in Micah 7:18. Here you will certainly need to keep your translation simple, but take time to offer a full explanation. Your ultimate interpretation may appear to be utterly unrelated to your text, as far as your audience is concerned, if you do not clearly understand what the text says and make it just as clear to them.

### Identify Historical and Geographical References

The last step in this particular process of interpretation will not apply to every text. But it will apply to a large number of the passages which you are called upon to interpret. If there are any historical or geographical references in your text, they must be carefully and accurately identified.

References to the names of people should be looked up in your concordance. Read the biblical material which gives additional information concerning them. Also, it would be wise to use your Bible dictionary and look up such persons as well. It will be surprising at how much insight such research will give you into the passage you are interpreting.

References to nations, battles, or to items of other historical significance should also be looked up in your concordance and your Bible dictionary. In addition, you should read the relevant material in your Old Testament history and in your archaeological references. It is important to learn all that you can of the significance of such references.

Finally, look up any cities, mountains, rivers, or other geographical references in your historical atlas. A good use of maps at this point with a thoughtful consideration of the details can add significant insight into what a text means. For example, the whole story of Elijah takes on new dimensions when it is read with maps before you. The same is true of Joshua's campaigns or the activities of the judges.

## Summary

In determining what the Old Testament text you are interpreting really says, there are several simple steps which we have outlined through which you must go. Be sure you have these mastered.

Step 1. *Consider the grammar.* Try to identify the kind of action described. Identify the time setting (tense) of the translation and seek to discover the reason for it. Decide upon the time or tense you will use if you disagree.

Step 2. *Consider the syntax.* Identify the verb, the subject, and the direct object (predicate). Note any divergence from expected word order, seeking to discover where the biblical author placed the emphasis. Identify the action of the verse. Try to visualize the picture, usually a moving picture, which the author was conveying.

Step 3. *Consider the punctuation.* Identify the simple phrases and clauses which were used to build the text. Determine how the punctuation affects your understanding of what the verse says.

Step 4. *Consider word usages.* Identify what the key words really meant to the Hebrews. What are the shades of meaning which show up in their usage in this and other passages? Further, identify any idioms which may be present. Seek to determine what they actually meant. Then identify the figures of speech. See what is really being communicated by the author through what was said.

Step 5. *Consider contemporary word meanings.* Do the English words used in your translation really communicate what the original author was trying to convey? Remember, the biblical writers were primarily communicating with ordinary people, not with theologians. Make sure that your translation does the same. *Use words which clearly indicate the meaning intended and which your audience will clearly understand.*

Step 6. *Identify historical and geographical references.* Are there any such references in your passage? What are they? In what way or ways do these references help you to understand what the text says? Can you locate all geographical references on your maps? If not, why not? Consider the nature of the terrain to which your passage refers. Does this add any insight to your understanding of what the passage says? If your passage has no such references, be sure to check the larger context for them. If they are there, follow this same procedure for understanding them.

## Practice Exercises

Actually, you should follow through with these steps any time you begin to interpret an Old Testament passage. As with determining the correct text, practice will help you develop both skill and speed. However, let me warn you, never let your desire for speed get in the way of doing a thorough job. Accuracy is essential. Speed is not.

To enable you to begin to develop both skill and familiarity, I have selected some passages which will help you without getting so involved in the process that you quit before you get through. In dealing with each of the following, be sure that you can answer the questions before going on to the next exercise.

1. Isaiah 11:1-5

(1) In what time is the action of the verbs? Do you agree with this timing? If not, how would you change it?

(2) Underline all of the verbs in your translation. In order to visualize the actions, describe in your own words what is going on.

(3) Do you note any special emphases from the syntax (sentence structure)? What? Why do you think the author was making these emphases?

(4) Are there any key words whose usages give special insights into meaning? What are they and what is the special meaning you see?

(5) Are there any idioms present? What meaning is carried by them?

(6) Do you see any figures of speech? How do they add to the meaning?

(7) Are there any words which really do not communicate to the class or congregation you envision? How would you change them to clarify the text?

## 2. Isaiah 40:31

This passage is of particular significance insofar as visualizing the action. Describe what the author was seeing here. Also, identify any figures of speech. What is being communicated by them?

## 3. Micah 6:6-8

This passage is of significance from the standpoint of syntax, punctuation, and word usage. Note the punctuation. Underline each question. As the questions are phrased, what answer is expected? In considering word usage, particularly look for significant figures of speech. What is their meaning? Finally, look at the things required of man by God in the last half of verse 8. Using your analytical concordance, see how these words or phrases are used elsewhere. Define each term in your own words. Be sure that you express this in simple terms.

## 4. Genesis 22:15

Actually, you will need to read Genesis 22:1-14 to familiarize yourself again with the story. In looking at the particular text, underline the verbs in Abraham's statement. What three actions were Abraham and Isaac going to perform? One of these anticipated actions is striking, in the light of the overall passage. Which is it? What do you think he was really saying? Try to locate the place on a map. If you can, consider other events which occurred in the same region.

When you have completed these exercises, then pick out several other passages and deal with them step-by-step, as we have outlined the process in the two preceding chapters. You might particularly enjoy doing Amos 1 and 2. When you begin to feel somewhat comfortable in applying these steps, then you are ready to move on to the next major step in interpretation.

### Note
1. Robert Polzin, *Biblical Structuralism* (Philadelphia: Fortress Press, 1977), pp. 6-7.

Sample Work Sheet
DETERMINING WHAT THE TEXT SAYS (OT)

Text: Book, chapter, and verses

1. Significant grammatical characteristics, including verb states


2. Significant syntactical relationships, including punctuation


3. Key words, including background and definitions


4. Significant historical and geographical references


5. Revised (if necessary) tentative translation

# Part 3
Preparing to Interpret
a New Testament Text

# 7

# Ensuring a Correct Text

With the New Testament as well as the Old, the first step in interpretation has to be the determination of what the text really says. Far too frequently, we who are called upon to interpret the New Testament select a version of a text from a particular translation simply because we like the way it sounds. A little thought will easily show just how wrong this procedure is. If we have the responsibility of interpreting God's Word to his people, we had better be as sure as possible that what we are interpreting is what the inspired author actually wrote, rather than what someone else thinks he should have written. We may do a good job of interpreting any particular passage, but if it is not what was originally inspired, we have wasted our time, our people's time, and God's time.

It is for this reason that the science of text criticism has arisen. As defined in chapter 5, *textual criticism is the science of determining as accurately as possible precisely what the inspired author wrote.* Here, too, before we can understand the techniques for doing this, we need to understand how the New Testament was transmitted. Although, in general, this process was quite similar to that of the transmission of the Old Testament, there is enough difference for it to be helpful for us to consider it separately. Before actually presenting this process, however, let me state clearly that the study of the New Testament text has given us great confidence in the accuracy of the process by which it was transmitted. Again, as in the Old Testament, the New Testament transmission process has allowed numerous textual variations to slip into the text. At the same time, it appears that God's Holy Spirit has so guided the process that these problems have, in general, been relatively minor. Further, we have been given enough tools by which to study the process and correct the difficulties so that we can approach the New Testament with the assurance that we have now come quite near the actual words which were originally written. We have an even greater assurance of the accuracy of our present text of the New Testament than we have of the Old.

### The Preservation and Transmission of the New Testament

Like the Old Testament, the New Testament was also preserved and passed on by copyists. This copying was done in one of two ways. Sometimes the copyist would look at the original and then write his copy. This allowed the possibility of one kind of copying mistake to get into the text, mistakes of sight. At other times, someone would read a manuscript to one or more copyists, who would then write the material. This allowed a different kind of scribal mistake, mistakes of sound.

Also, more frequently than in Old Testament manuscripts, material was recorded without spaces between words or sentences. Furthermore, when a scribe got to the end of the line, he might break off right in the middle of a word, with no indication that he had done so. This allowed for mistakes of understanding to creep into the text as it was used by future copyists. It should be noted that this did not create as many problems for New Testament copyists as it had for Old Testament copyists, since vowels were also present. Consider the following illustration.

ForGodsolovedtheworldthathegavehisonlySonthatwhoeverbeliev
esinhimshouldnotperishbuthaveeternallifeForGodsenttheSonintot
heworldnottocondemntheworldbutthattheworldmightbesavedthro
oughhim

Two things are immediately obvious. First, this is relatively easy to read. Second, it does open up possibilities of misunderstanding.

Also, corrections and/or marginal notes made on any manuscript created problems for future copyists. They then had to decide if it indicated a correction which needed to be inserted or a note which should not be copied. In addition, variations made in the text by one copyist were automatically picked up by later copyists, thus adding to the problems.

There are two other major differences between the copies made of the Old Testament and those of the New Testament. First, New Testament copyists, at least at the first, were not usually professional scribes. Their very lack of skill thus added to the potential for variations. Furthermore, copies of New Testament books and of the entire New Testament were much more numerous than those of the Old Testament. Copies were usually provided for every church, and old manuscripts were not destroyed when new ones were made.

Through the process of copying, families of manuscripts began to arise. To illustrate this, consider the following chart.

|  | *Original Manuscript* | |
| --- | --- | --- |
| (2 copies made) | *COPY A* (0 variations) | *COPY B* (3 variations) |
| (next copies) | *A-1* (5 variations) | *B-1* (1 variation) |
| (next copies) | *A-2* (3, 8 total) | *B-2* (4, 5 total) |
| (next copies) | *A-3* (7, 15 total) | *B-3* (2, 7 total) |
| (next copies) | *A-4* (4, 19 total) | *B-4* (2, 9 total) |
| (next copies) | *A-5* (4, 23 total) | *B-5* (1, 10 total) |

This chart illustrates two things. First, copies made of copies merely increase the total number of textual variations in the latest or newest manuscript in any family of copies. Second, if an archaeologist had discovered copy *A-3* and *B-5*, even though *A-3* is considerably older and nearer the original, *B-5* has far less variations in it. Thus, in evaluating the relative value of manuscripts, the textual critic must not only consider the age of manuscripts but their family as well. Some manuscript families show much greater care in copying than others do.

### Categories of Textual Problems in the New Testament

It is against this background of the processes and dynamics involved in copying that we are able to understand the nature and types of textual variations which have crept into our New Testament manuscripts during the centuries of copying. These are, in general, identical to the kinds of scribal glosses which crept into Old Testament transmission and which were noted in chapter 5. However, to simplify your use of this book, I will repeat them here, making particular note of how these affect our understanding of New Testament textual studies.

### Accidents in Copying

As we have already seen, variations did get into New Testament manuscripts through the centuries of their copying. By far the overwhelming number of these are simply accidental. While these are easy to demonstrate to a person who reads Greek, I shall try to illustrate them with examples in English.

A significant number of scribal glosses can be classified simply as *slips of the pen.* Letters which are similar in shape can be left unclear by a scribe. For example, if the first letter of "nun" is made sloppily, it could be understood as "run," radically changing a meaning. This kind of slip of the pen occurred quite frequently in early New Testament manuscripts.

Closely related to this in some ways are *mistakes of the eye.* These show up first when a scribe misunderstood letters which are similar in shape. It is sometimes difficult to determine with this kind of mistake whether it was a slip of the pen or simply a problem of the eye. However, another kind of misjudgment of the eye occurred when a scribe allowed his eye to shift from a word or phrase in one verse to a similar word or phrase in the next. For example, consider the following.

> In the beginning was the Word, and the Word was *with God*, and the Word was God. He was in the beginning *with God*; all things were made through him, and without him was not anything made that was made (John 1:1-3, italics mine).

If a scribe, copying this, allowed his eye to slip from the first "with God" to the second, the copy could come out like this.

> In the beginning was the Word, and the Word was with God, all things were made through him, and without him was not anything made that was made.

Such a slip would have left out the tremendous assertion that "the Word was God," radically changing the message and impact of these verses.

A third type of mistake of the eye occurred when a scribe might go back and copy the same expression twice. This would not occur if the scribe were thinking about what he was copying. But when the process became mechanical enough, scribes could and did make such copying mistakes.

Another major type of accidental slip is classified as *mistakes of the ear.* This obviously would occur when someone was reading a manuscript to the copyist. Consider the fact that some different words have identical sounds, such as "led" and "lead," while others can sound alike when poorly pronounced, such as "coal" and "cold." To consider someone's "bad cold" might be understood as evaluating his "bad coal," the poor fuel he was selling.

In addition to these kinds of textual variations, in the New Testament there were also *mistakes of understanding or mistakes due to confusion.* These show up in the process of trying to properly separate words when they had been written without separation or punctuation. They also show up when a scribe was forced to decide whether or not a marginal note was an actual correction of a text made by the original copyist or some explanation just inserted there to clarify or explain. In such cases, the scribe was forced to make a decision as to which it was. If he made the wrong decision, a variation had gotten into the text.

Finally, in the category of accidents in copying in the New Testament text, there are some which are simply *unclassifiable variations.* It would just appear that such variations got into the text through some lapse of mind on the part of the copyists. These are few in number and, while not classifiable, can usually be quite easily detected and corrected on the basis of the textual information which we have.

## Deliberate Alterations

Although not nearly as frequent as the accidents in copying, there is evidence of some deliberate alterations which have been made in copying New Testament manuscripts. These result in five kinds of textual variations.

There are those changes which a scribe made with the intention of *making a passage conform to the general context.* First, consider that in John 7:8 Jesus said, "I am not going up to this feast." But later, Jesus did go up to the feast, apparently changing his mind (John 7:10). Somewhere along the way in copying this passage, a scribe added the word *yet* to Jesus' statement, making it read "I am not yet going up to this feast." (See the KJV.)

Second, a scribe might occasionally make alterations, *correcting a text.* Poor Greek might be turned into good Greek. The Book of Revelation, for example, is written in simple Greek with frequent use of incorrect case endings, indicating that the human author was not a brilliant linguist. Many scribes, in copying this material, would correct the case endings much as a teacher might correct a pupil's paper. This has given rise to multiple variations of case endings.

Third, occasionally corrections seem to have been made for the purpose of *giving greater dignity or honor to Jesus.* Consider the fact that in Galatians 6:17, Paul wrote, "I bear on my body the marks of Jesus." In numerous manuscripts this has been changed to read "our Lord Jesus Christ," or "Christ," or "Lord Jesus," or "the Lord Jesus Christ."

Fourth, there are also indications that sometimes *scribes changed a text for the purpose of making it conform to other accounts of the same event.* Paul, telling of his conversion in Acts, states that Jesus said to him, "It hurts you to kick against the goads" (26:14). In the record of this event in Acts 9:4, this particular statement was not recorded in the best manuscripts, but it was inserted in some manuscripts. The fact that it was not recorded in Acts 9:4 did not mean that it did not happen. It just was not recorded there originally.

Fifth, there are those places where an ancient scribe added a word, a phrase, or an entire paragraph, simply *supplying additional information* which they thought should have been included by the original author. The best example of this is the story of the woman caught in the act of adultery and brought to Jesus for judgment (John 7:53 to 8:11). This entire episode simply is not in the best manuscripts. Although it certainly sounds exactly like what Jesus would have done, and quite likely is something he did do, it was not originally recorded by the author of the Fourth Gospel.

In surveying the kinds of textual variations which have crept into the New Testament, we come to a similar conclusion as that in chapter 5 where we considered the textual variations of the Old Testament. First, the persons who copied the ancient manuscripts of the New Testament were human, making precisely the same kinds of mistakes which competent copyists make today in copying written material. But second, and far more important, the variations which did get into the ancient copies of the New Testament are generally identifiable and correctable. It is this fact which demands that we give a brief consideration to the actual process by which New Testament textual experts attempt to determine the most accurate text of the New Testament.

### The Nature of New Testament Textual Studies

When we have understood the processes by which textual variations got into the New Testament text, we are just about ready to try to understand the techniques by which textual scholars seek to determine the original. However, we must first consider the resources which are available to those who spend their lives in analyzing the New Testament text.

### *The Resources Available*

There are many, many more materials available for the New Testament textual critic than there are for the Old Testament scholar. This very multiplicity of resources makes the task at first seem more formidable. On the other hand, this same multiplicity makes the results of such studies far more assured for the New Testament. These resource materials are usually classified into three basic subdivisions.

By far the most important type of ancient manuscripts which the New Testament text critic has available are actual *manuscripts of the Greek New Testament, or at least of some part of it*. There are four kinds of these which I have listed in order of their importance.

(1) Uncial manuscripts of the Greek New Testament are written in capital letters, usually on lambskin (vellum). More than two hundred and sixty of these have been discovered, and a significant portion of them are relatively complete. The earliest of these apear to be dated about AD 350.

(2) Papyrus fragments of the Greek New Testament represent portions of the New Testament which have been found written on papyrus. These are usually older than the uncials, but due to the fact that they are usually only portions of the New Testament, they are not of as much total value as the uncials. There are at least 85 of these known at present. Some of them are very small, containing only an insignificant fragment, while others are more extensive. Every book in the New Testament is represented among the papyri (plural of papyrus) except 1 and 2 Timothy. One of these ancient portions is dated in the early part of the second century, very close to the actual date of its original writing.

(3) Miniscule manuscripts of the Greek New Testament are written in small letters, usually joined together in a form of cursive handwriting. There are at least 2,750 of these which are known to exist. This kind of writing came into use about the ninth or tenth century. Although they are not nearly as old as the uncials, they frequently appear to represent a copy of a text older than that from which the uncials were copied. It must be noted that a manuscript is as good as its copyist and the original from which it was copied. A more recent copy of a good manuscript is better than an older copy which was poorly made.

(4) Lectionaries of ancient churches contained Scriptures which had been copied to be read in worship services. These generally

appear to be quite secondary in value. However, there are more than 2,100 of these known.

In addition to these resources for the New Testament text critic, the second basic classification of resources is the many *quotations from the New Testament which are contained in the writings of the Church Fathers.* (These were the leaders, preachers, and spokesmen of the early Christian communities. The study of their writings is usually called Patristics.) These writings are extensive, and their quotations are numerous. In fact, they are so abundant that it has been estimated that almost the entire New Testament could be reconstructed from these writings alone. Although not as important a resource as actual copies of the New Testament, they are of great value in helping scholars determine which text (or text family) was in use in a particular place at a particular time.

The third major classification of resources for the New Testament textual critic is *copies of ancient translations of the New Testament in other languages.* There are more than thirteen thousand of these. Among the more important are translations into Coptic (Egyptian), Syriac, Latin, and Ethiopic. Although such translations are not as useful as the other resources for determining the best text, they are a witness to what was actually contained in the New Testament. Many of these clearly were translated from Greek manuscripts older than any which we now possess. While of great significance, the very nature of translations means that they can seldom be used as the final evidence of what an ancient passage originally said.

From these resources, the New Testament textual critic amasses the evidence to be used in trying to reconstruct what the original manuscripts actually contained. At this point, we can now consider and understand the methods which such biblical students apply to their work.

### The Methods of New Testament Textual Studies

In beginning the task of determining the best or most accurate text of any New Testament passage, the textual critics *compare ancient manuscripts,* seeking to identify those which are usually most reliable.

This process is begun by grouping those manuscripts together which appear to have common ancestry. Then by comparison and systematic analysis, the text critics are usually able to determine which family of copies is most reliable. (For those interested in the details of this process, a good book on New Testament text criticism will be helpful. For our purposes here, suffice it to say that it can be done and that there is a fairly clear distinction between the accuracy of the various manuscript families.) With the present state of New Testament textual studies, this is often the only step needed in determining the most probable text among the possible variants. The variant which appears in the most reliable family of manuscripts is most likely the correct one. However, this conclusion must always be considered as tentative until other aspects are considered. It is these to which we must now direct our attention.

Through the years of studying the various texts and versions of the New Testament, a set of principles or rules has been developed which have given good results in *determining the best variant* of any text. In general, these steps are similar to those in Old Testament textual criticism. However, there are some differences. Therefore we are considering them separately. Furthermore, for those interpreters who know no Greek, they are completely in the hands of the scholars. This applies to most interpreters, but it is not an irretrievable loss.

However, even if you cannot read Greek, it is wise at least to know something of the process by which textual critics make such decisions. Those interpreters who can read Greek can make such decisions on their own, but you must be warned that no interpreter can become an expert at this overnight. As with anything else of value, only much study and practice can develop the skills needed to become a textual critic who can be confident of his work. There are five basic principles which a New Testament textual critic usually applies.

1. *The rule of meaning.* We begin with the assumption that God did not inspire nonsense. Furthermore, we also assume that no human author would have written a passage which made no sense. Therefore, a passage should make sense. However, it should be noted that just because we do not understand a passage does not

mean that it did not originally make sense. It may be our own ignorance of the meaning of words or phrases or our lack of knowledge of customs, backgrounds, geography, and such which make a passage appear to make no sense. This principle is applied, but it must always be tempered with caution. New discoveries might make sense of an apparently nonsensical passage.

2. *The rule of difficulty.* Although we can certainly assume that the original passage made sense, we can also assume that if some scribe has altered a passage, he did so in order to make a difficult passage simpler. Therefore, we usually assume that the more difficult variant is probably the original.

3. *The rule of explanation.* It is frequently quite easy to see why a copyist might have changed one reading into another, but impossible to see why he would have gone the other way. In this case, the passage which most easily explains the development of the other is to be preferred. However, we must be warned that this is an attempt to get into the mind of a copyist, which is always quite subjective. We can never be sure just how someone else's mind might have worked.

4. *The rule of shortness.* In general, textual critics assume that if an alteration occurred in a passage, it would have been an attempt to explain it and, therefore, would have made it longer, using more words. Again, this is also rather subjective and must be applied with care.

5. *The rule of circumstance.* The variant which fits best into the circumstances of the author or the book is to be preferred. Each writer in the New Testament has his own particular style, vocabulary, and particular way of expressing himself. It is sometimes even possible to determine which variant best fits into the personality of the author. This is the most subjective rule of all and, therefore, is the most difficult to apply with certainty.

### The Results of New Testament Textual Studies

As has been noted earlier, the results of New Testament text criticism have given us a growing assurance of the accuracy of our present text. The achievements of the textual critics have been widely accepted. There is almost no doubt that we have identified the basically authentic text of the New Testament. In the overwhelming majority of cases, we can be certain that we have the original material precisely as it was originally written. In those verses where there may still be some doubt as to the absolutely exact words of the original, no significant teaching or basic doctrine is in question. There are essentially only matters of detail yet to be settled. Furthermore, even though the science of text criticism had not developed at the time, even the Greek text used by the King James translators has been demonstrated to be an acceptable text. Once again, the evidence indicates that while God allowed the copiers of the text to be human and to make human mistakes, he still so undergirded the process that his revelation can be clearly understood.

## Arriving at a Tentative Translation

Since most Christians cannot use Greek, you as an interpreter need a procedure by which the actual wording of a text can be determined with reasonable assurance. Obviously, you and I usually begin with an English translation. But this process cannot be depended upon if we just use one such translation. The very nature of translating makes such a procedure questionable. Therefore, just as we did with the Old Testament, we will need to follow a series of steps which will enable us to arrive at a translation which can be depended upon. We must select at least three translations from which to work. I will use the RSV and KJV, along with either the NASB or the NEB, and sometimes both. Although you may wish to use a different translation for your third one, I still strongly suggest that you do use the RSV and the KJV as your first two. The following steps should help you to achieve the desired results. (It should be noted that these steps are identical to those listed for the Old Testament. I am repeating them here for your ease in using this procedure.)

Step 1. *Arrange the biblical material in a manner which will most easily facilitate comparison.* You can do this by arranging the material either in parallel lines or in parallel columns. You should try both to see which appears to be easiest for you. Due to the length and involvement of many New Testament sentences, I find that parallel lines are far more effective for me than parallel columns. If you can read Greek, you should begin with the Greek, then your own translation, then the translations which you have selected. Also, variants noted in your Greek text should be listed along with your translation. For most of us who do not use Greek, you will have three or four lines (or columns) from the selected translations, along with a fourth or fifth giving the alternate translations suggested in the marginal notes.

Step 2. *Underline the various words and phrases in your translations which differ from one another.* In your own work, you might find that using a different color pencil or pen for adjacent variations will help keep things sorted out more effectively. In the examples which follow, these differences will be indicated with bold type. In identifying differences, you can ignore those which are caused by differences in old English and in modern English, such as "thou" and "you." You can also ignore difference in punctuation at this point, unless such differences significantly alter the meaning.

Step 3. *Consider the differences between the various translations.* At this point you should seriously question whether the differences are really significant or whether the various translators are merely substituting synonymous expressions. In order to make this easier, you should refer to a Bible dictionary and to an English dictionary. Be sure that you actually know what the words really mean. One or two good commentaries can be of value here in helping you to evaluate the word meanings and the translators' difficulties.

Step 4. *Make a tentative translation of the verse for yourself.* As you do this step, keep in mind the audience for whom you are making the translation. Seek to use words which will be easily understood by the particular group to whom you will be interpreting the passage. Furthermore, as you make your decisions, you can apply the rules for evaluating textual differences which we considered earlier in the chapter. Never decide to use a word or a phrase just because it happens to agree with your preconceived ideas. We must be careful to try to discover exactly what the Bible is really saying, rather than what we want it to say.

Step 5. *Keep reminding yourself that your translation is only tentative.* In progressing through the remaining steps of interpretation, you may discover that you need to modify or correct your translation. You should never accept a translation as final until you have completed the entire task of interpretation. As we have noted on several occasions, no interpretation is ever better than the translation from which it comes. Therefore, if your further study should make you realize that your translation needs to be altered, alter it! Do not get locked in to an incorrect translation.

This sounds like hard work, and it is. But if we believe that we are interpreting the very words of life to people, then no effort should be considered too difficult. As you practice these procedures, the task will become somewhat easier, but it will never become easy. However, it is only as we approach the Bible seriously, grappling with its real message, that we shall have its rich treasures unlocked for us. Furthermore, it is only then that we shall be able to open its riches for others.

## Selected Examples

In order to begin to learn how to apply the preceding steps, we will now consider some specific examples. To make this more typical, I have not put in either the Greek or my own translation. I am seeking to do this precisely as most people would have to do it. Numbers in parentheses are guides to the discussions of the differences in the translations.

1. Romans 5:1-2

KJV:     Therefore being justified by faith,
RSV:     Therefore, **since** we are justified by faith,
NEB:     Therefore, **now** that we have been justified (1) through
            faith,

| NASB: | Therefore having been justified by faith, |
|---|---|
| KJV: | *we have* peace with God |
| RSV: | *we have* peace with God |
| NEB: | *let us continue* at peace with God |
| NASB: | *we have* peace with God |
| Variant | *let us . . .* (2) |

| KJV: | through our Lord Jesus Christ: |
|---|---|
| RSV: | through our Lord Jesus Christ. |
| NEB: | through our Lord Jesus Christ, |
| NASB: | through our Lord Jesus Christ, |

| KJV: | *By whom* also we have *access by faith* (3,4,5) |
|---|---|
| RSV: | *Through him* we have *obtained access* |
| NEB: | *through whom* we have been *allowed to enter* |
| NASB: | *through whom* also we have *obtained* our *intro-duction by faith* |
| Variant: | *. . . by faith* |

| KJV: | into this grace wherein we stand, |
|---|---|
| RSV: | to this grace in which we stand, |
| NEB: | *the sphere of God's grace,* where we *now* stand. (6,7) |
| NASB: | into this grace in which we stand; |

| KJV: | and *rejoice* in hope of the glory of God. (8) |
|---|---|
| RSV: | and we *rejoice* in *our* hope *of sharing* the glory of God. (9,10) |
| NEB: | *Let us exult* in *the* hope of *the divine splendour that is to be ours.* (11) |
| NASB: | and *we exult* in hope of the glory of God. |
| Variant: | and *let us exult . . .* |

(1) *Now, since,* or neither one? None of the versions has a textual note indicating any problem. Furthermore, both added words appear to be a translator's attempt to clarify a difficult expression. I would reject both.

(2) *We have* or *let us*? The textual notes in RSV, NEB, and NASB indicate that there is manuscript evidence for both. The

question is: did Paul make a simple declaration that since we have been justified, we now have peace with God, or is it an exhortation to enter into or to continue in God's peace? It would appear to me that *we have* is to be preferred, although a fairly good case can be established for the alternative.

(3) *By whom, through whom,* or *through him*? There appears to be very little difference. I accept *through whom*.

(4) *Access* is rendered four different ways. Each appears to be an attempt to clarify the shorter expression. I accept the simple *we have access*.

(5) *By faith* appears to be a later addition for clarification. It appears to me that the shorter, simpler statement is to be preferred. There is no doubt but that *by faith* was implied by Paul, but it would appear that he really did not write it that way.

(6) *The sphere of* certainly appears to be an enlargement upon the original text and is to be rejected.

(7) *Now* appears to be the same kind of an enlargement.

(8) *Rejoice, exult,* or *let us exult*? *Let us exult* is indicated as a possible textual variant. Since it is the larger expression and appears to be a clarification, I would reject it as a part of the original. Furthermore, *exult* and *rejoice* appear to be alternate translations of the same expression. Since to me, *exult* carries a sense of pride to which it does not appear Paul was referring, I would accept the simple *rejoice*.

(9) *Our hope, the hope,* or simply *hope*? It would appear that both *our* and *the* have been supplied by the translators to clarify. I would prefer to accept the shorter and blunter *hope*.

(10) *Of sharing* clearly appears to be a translator's enlargement and is to be rejected.

(11) *The divine splendour that is to be ours* also appears to be a place where the translators let their fanciful words run away with them.

**Tentative Translation:** Therefore being justified by faith we have peace with God through our Lord Jesus Christ, through whom we have access to this grace in which we stand, and rejoice in hope of the glory of God. (Note: If you have carefully followed each step of this process, you will have noted that the NEB has had a very real tendency to enlarge and to be rather free with its additions. This appears to be a pattern throughout.)

2. John 7:8

| KJV: | Go *ye* up unto this *feast*: |
| RSV: | Go to the *feast yourselves*; |
| NEB: | Go to the *festival yourselves*; |
| NASB: | Go up to the *feast yourselves;* (1) |

| KJV: | I go not up *yet* unto this *feast*; |
| RSV: | I am not going up to this *feast*, |
| NEB: | I am not going up to this *festival* |
| NASB: | I do not go up to this *feast* |
| Variant: | . . . going up *yet* . . . (2,3) |

| KJV: | *for my* time is not yet *full* come. |
| RSV: | *for my* time has not yet *fully* come. |
| NEB: | *because the right time for me* has not yet come. |
| NASB: | *because My time* has not yet *fully* come. (4,5,6) |

(1) The difference between *ye* and *yourselves* is that the former is old English and is no longer in popular use. *Feast* and *festival* are merely variations of the same word. The former is probably more American English while the latter is more British English. I would prefer "Go up to the feast yourselves."

(2) There is a problem with the addition or deletion of *yet*. Since the same chapter says later that Jesus did go up to the feast (v. 10), it is easy to understand why a copyist would have added the *yet* to clarify a difficult situation. It is difficult to understand why he would have left it out, if it had originally been there. The probability is that *yet* was not in the original text.

(3) The same problem of *feast* and *festival* shows up here also. Again, I reject the use of *festival* for American audiences.

(4) *For* or *because*? Actually there is little difference. Either could be satisfactorily used.

(5) *My time* or *the right time for me*? Clearly, here again the

NEB has supplied a large number of unnecessary words. There might be a question as to whether or not the pronoun ought to be capitalized. Capitalization is frequently used by translators when they believe the pronoun refers to God. However, in many cases this is a translator's judgment which might be disputed. Since the Greek normally makes no differentiation, it is probably wise not to capitalize. However, if it shows greater reverence to God in your mind, there is no difficulty if you should decide to capitalize it.

(6) *Full* or *fully*? To bring the translation into good modern English, the *fully* form should be used, for we normally do not use "full" as an adverb today.

**Tentative Translation:** Go up to feast yourselves. I am not going to this feast, for my time has not yet fully come.

## Practice Exercises

The only way to develop any kind of skill in doing this is to do it yourself. Although more examples could be given, they would not be of nearly the value of you doing this for yourself. If you will do the following exercises as I have done the examples, going through the step-by-step procedure, you will achieve results with which you can be satisfied. In beginning this process, I will suggest several passages which ought not to be too difficult, but which will offer some challenge.

You might begin by trying Luke 8:43. As you work with it, remember that Luke was a physician. You might also compare this with Matthew 9:20 and Mark 5:26. Carefully consider what you might have expected Luke to record.

Next, turn to Romans 8:28. In dealing with this, try to determine in your own mind how the variants might have come about. It will also be helpful for you to note that the basic meaning of the passage is hardly changed, regardless of which variant you accept.

Moving from these specific suggestions to random selections, you would probably find it wise to begin by focusing your attention upon several random passages where the RSV actually lists a variant in the marginal notes. After dealing with a few like this, making sure that they are scattered through the Gospels, the Epistles, and Acts, it would probably be wise to settle down and focus your attention upon a particular book. You might find Colossians a good one. In order to aid you in this task, use the sample worksheet. It is like the one which is at the end of chapter 5.

Sample Work Sheet
ARRIVING AT A TENTATIVE TRANSLATION

Text: Book, chapter, and verses

1. Arrange the text in parallel lines. Underline significant differences.

2. Evaluate the differences. List reasons for your decisions.

3. Tentative Translation. (Let your form show prose or poetry.)

# 8
# Determining What the Text Says

In trying to determine precisely what a New Testament text says, the same advice is applicable here that was offered in regard to the Old Testament (ch. 6). No interpretation of a biblical passage can possibly be any better than the accuracy of the translation which you are using. A poor translation can only result in a poor interpretation. But, and this must be clearly understood, a good translation does not necessarily mean that you will have a good interpretation. It only means that you have now opened the door to that possibility.

To this point, we have arrived at a tentative translation of the passage which we wish to interpret. As a matter of fact, all we really have in our tentative New Testament translation is a collection of words which are far more involved and possibly make less sense than a tentative Old Testament translation. Therefore, it is even more important for anyone who would properly interpret the New Testament to come to grips with precisely what the text says. This involves grammar, syntax, word usages and meanings, and the identification of historical, geographical, and literary references.

Here also, there are some warnings of which we need to be aware. First, sentences in the New Testament are frequently much longer, far more involved and complex, and, therefore, far more difficult to understand and to interpret than Old Testament sentences. This is even more true in Paul's writings than in the Gospels. To do a good job of interpretation of a New Testament text will require constant attention to matters of grammar and syntax. Probably more interpretation of the New Testament fails at this point than anywhere else.

Second, there is hardly any basis in the New Testament for the

**143**

assumption by some persons that New Testament interpretation is subjective. There are clearly places where a subjective judgment must be rendered as to what an English sentence might say. Consider the child who said, "Mother would like to relax Daddy." This could be understood as the child telling his father that "Mother would like to relax." Perhaps she has had a trying day and just needs to sit down and rest for a while. On the other hand, it might be that the father has just come in from a trying day and the child is saying that his mother would like to massage his father's neck. From the English, either interpretation is possible. But the Greek is generally much more precise than this. Word endings will indicate whether "Daddy" is the object of the verb "to relax" or not. Thus, even though some subjectivity enters into interpretation, determining actual sentence structure is usually much more objective. A good translator will use punctuation to help clarify.

The third warning focuses upon your own language skills. Since New Testament sentences do get so involved, you will need to make every effort to become a good student of English grammar and syntax. You certainly need to know how to express yourself clearly and accurately. But, as you improve your skills in this area, you will be better able to analyze the complex sentences of the New Testament to understand precisely what is being said. God obviously revealed and inspired his word to communicate truth, not to hide it. Therefore, we must pursue this aspect of our procedure with the care necessary to determine precisely what the inspired text says. Anything less than our best at this point is poor stewardship of our talents and of God's gift of his Word.

Certainly, we have all seen cases in which God's Spirit has convicted people in spite of poor interpretation. On the other hand, we have also seen poor interpretation keep people from even considering the claims of the gospel. We must not be guilty of allowing this to happen with us.

### Consider the Grammar and Syntax

The basic grammar and syntax of the Greek New Testament is similar to English. Therefore, there is not as much difference between the two as there is between Hebrew and English. This, however, must not be allowed to lull us into a sense of false security. Such a feeling can absolutely destroy the care with which we proceed. This, in turn, can destroy the accuracy of our interpretation.

## *Identify the Parts of Speech*

Before you can begin to understand what a sentence really says, you must first identify the various parts of speech in the sentence. This is especially difficult for many of us, since the American educational system has seriously neglected this for a generation or more. However, just because it has been neglected does not mean that it is unimportant. (If your knowledge of English grammar and syntax is particularly weak, an investment in a good handbook of English grammar would be quite helpful. Not only would it help you to understand a verse, it will help you to communicate your interpretation clearly and with precision.) There are six basic parts of speech with which you ought to be familiar and which you ought to be able to recognize. Let us consider them briefly.

1. *The subject.* The subject may be a noun, a pronoun, a phrase, or a clause, and their modifiers. It is used to identify the actor, or with passive verbs, the one (or thing) acted upon. Also, the subject may identify anything or anyone about whom a statement is made or a question is asked.

2. *The verb (or predicate).* The verb expresses action or existence. It may occur as a simple word or a verbal phrase and may include modifiers or coordinating particles. The verb not only indicates action or existence, it may also indicate a kind of action, the time of an action, or the very nature of the subject.

3. *The object.* The object may also be a noun, a pronoun, or a clause, along with their modifiers. It may identify the thing or the person acted upon, and thus be a direct object. It may also identify something or someone who benefited by the action, and thus be an indirect object.

Example: Consider the simple sentence: "She gave the ball to him." "She" is the subject. "Gave" is the verb, communicating action. "The ball" is the direct object, since it was acted upon; it was literally moved from one person to another. "Him" is the indirect object, since he received the ball, being the beneficiary of the action.

4. *The adjective.* The adjective may be a word, a phrase, or a clause which describes either the subject or the object. It usually tells which one or what kind.

5. *The adverb.* The adverb may also be a word, a phrase, or a clause which modifies the verb and usually tells how, when, where, why, or how much. Note: Both adverbs and adjectives are classified as modifiers.

6. *The connectors.* The connectors are usually very short words identified as prepositions, relative pronouns, and conjunctions. They serve to indicate coordination or subordination.

Example: Enlarging our earlier sentence, we now have: "She quickly gave the red ball to him." "She," "gave," "ball," and "him" are still the same. "Quickly" is an adverb, modifying the verb by telling how she gave the ball. "Red" is an adjective, describing the kind of ball which was given. "To" is actually a connector. In this case it is a preposition.

This may all seem quite needless. To the contrary, it becomes very important. The more involved a sentence becomes, the more important this process is. It is only by following this kind of discipline that you can begin to be sure just what a sentence really says. The definitions and listings which I have given are adequate to get you started on the process and to guide you as you proceed. However, if you wish to become an expert, you will need to enlarge this list significantly. It is here that a good English grammar will be helpful.

Furthermore, if you do know how to diagram a sentence, you will find that this is frequently the best process for getting to understand what a New Testament sentence really says. For those who do not know how to do this, it is far too involved to go into here. (Again, to master the skill of sentence diagraming, I refer you to a good grammar book. However, check the book carefully before you buy it. Not every English grammar goes into sentence diagraming.)

### Determine Relationships

Once you have identified the various parts of speech in the sentence which you wish to interpret, then you need to determine the relationships of the various words to one another. It is here that sentence diagraming could prove most helpful. But if you do not have that skill, then what do you do? You carefully analyze the relationship between various words of the sentence. The study of the relationship of the various parts of speech in a sentence to one another is called syntax.

The normal word order in a sentence is: the subject (and its modifiers, if any) followed by the verb (and its modifiers, if any) followed by the direct object (and its modifiers, if any) followed by the indirect object (and its modifiers, if any). Furthermore, any one or all of these can be made compound by the addition of a parallel expression tied in by the use of a conjunction. Sentence word order can be altered for emphasis.

It is important for the interpreter to identify the various parts of speech in the sentence in order to be able to properly understand what the writer or speaker was seeking to communicate. You do not have to be an expert grammarian to be a good interpreter. But you cannot be a good interpreter and be a poor grammarian. God's truth is communicated through language, and language requires a knowledge of grammar and syntax if we are going to understand it. It is just that simple.

There is one major difference between English verbs and Greek verbs which we must note. The Greek language developed a special verb tense to indicate punctiliar or point action (aorist). This was to be understood as clearly different from linear or durative action. In many situations it is already clear. "To blink an eye" clearly refers to one action which happened at a specific point in time. On the other hand, "to live a life" just as clearly refers to an action which is ongoing, and, therefore, is linear or durative.

Furthermore, there are some verb forms which indicate action which is completed. Note, however, that this is not normally as significant in the Greek as it is in the Hebrew. Again, some English translations clearly indicate that action is completed. In the sentence, "He went to town and bought a hat," the verb "went" is clearly completed.

However, this entire process of identifying the kind of action can get quite involved. Frequently, for example, an action which might appear to us to be linear is used in the Greek tense which indicates that the author was viewing it from a point. Paul wrote in Romans 5:12, "all men sinned," but the Greek verb indicates that he was talking about point action. Here, he was looking at all the sin of all mankind as a whole, not all of the individual sins of each of us. Obviously, this kind of information is not available to you simply through the reading of the English text. Since you probably cannot read Greek, you must use a good commentary which will tell you about the kind of action when it is significant.

Furthermore, an aid to understanding the syntax in a sentence can be found in the punctuation. A good translator will utilize punctuation frequently to communicate some aspects of Greek grammar and syntax. Pay attention to the punctuation. Far too often than should occur, an interpretation is ruined by the interpreter failing to notice the punctuation.

It is only as you and I carefully identify the various parts of speech in a sentence and determine their relationships to one another that we shall be able to begin to understand what the author was saying. Be warned again, this is only a beginning.

## Consider Word Usages

Once we have understood how the inspired author put a sentence together, then we are ready to move on to the next step of considering the meaning of particular words and phrases in the New Testament. At this point, we need to recognize that our task is that of discovering what a word or phrase meant in New Testament times. What we should never forget (but often fail to remember) is that words have a history. The meaning of words change with their usages. For example, when I was a boy, if someone said, "That's tough!" it meant that some situation was quite difficult to handle. By the time that I had teenage children, the same expression meant that something was just great, it was wonderful. Thus, the interpreter must try to understand just what a word or phrase meant to the speaker or writer and to his audience.

It is important to accept that at this point our task is that of an explorer. When Columbus first came to the New World, he forced his own preconceptions upon what he had done and decided that he had found a new route to India. As we clearly know, he was wrong. Instead, he had found a new continent. If we force our own preconceptions upon what words meant to the people of the New Testament times, we may wind up just as wrong. For Columbus, his erroneous misconceptions were not a matter of life and death. Since the Bible does deal with eternal issues, an error on our part can be a matter of life and death. In order to begin to discover what a word meant, we must examine word usages. This includes both usages in the New Testament and in the New Testament world.

The primary tool for this is an analytical concordance. Theological wordbooks and commentaries which emphasize word studies are also helpful at this point. The analytical concordance will help you to see exactly how a particular word was used in every passage in which it occurs in the New Testament. It may also help you to discover how similar ideas were expressed and understood in the Old Testament. Furthermore, the analytical concordance will keep you from confusing two different Greek words which might have the same English translation. For example, five different Greek words are translated as *iniquity*. You, as an interpreter, must seek to determine precisely what each word meant, and not just what the English word *iniquity* means.

We begin doing this by examining all of the passages where identical words for *iniquity* appear. It is likely that where we have a reasonable number of references we might be able to discover what the particular meaning of each of these words was. Furthermore, by checking in the back of the analytical concordance, we can discover what additional ways a particular Greek word was translated. If we are going to be thorough in our investigation, we must also check out each of these passages.

After you have actually considered the various biblical references, then you should turn to your commentaries and theological word-books. But do not do this until you have sought to understand the usages first from your own investigation. These additional tools may add some insights in the dimension of extrabiblical uses of the word. They probably will not tell you anything about the usage in the Bible which you have not already found out for yourself. You should not become dependent upon these other helps when it is not necessary. They are of real value, but can become a crutch. Trust God's leadership of your own mind.

## Consider Word Meanings

Once you have discovered how a word or phrase was used in the New Testament, you are now ready to fully "discover" what its meaning was. This is usually done by drawing together every passage where a word is used, studying how it is used in each, considering how it was used outside the New Testament, and evaluating these in the light of the word's origin (its etymology). Sometimes the word's origin may shed no light on the New Testament uses of a word, but it cannot be ignored.

At this point, you are almost ready to determine what the specific word or phrase under study means. But before we go further, let me point out some major dangers.

1. Not all words can be taken literally. Ancient people, just like modern people, used figures of speech. We must seek to identify figures of speech and to understand them. For example, in John 1:4, we are told that "the life was the light of men." Now "light" is clearly used here as a figure of speech. The "life" of which John wrote illuminates our lives, scattering the darkness of sin, grief, and despair.

2. We cannot assume that an ancient word meant the same thing in the New Testament as it does in the modern world. A contempo-

rary dictionary is a poor tool for finding out what a biblical writer meant when he used any particular word. Furthermore, the way we use words in churches today is often far removed from what biblical writers meant with the same word. We use *apostle* as generally referring to one of the twelve. In the New Testament, an apostle was one who had been sent with a message. In reality, the modern word *missionary* is probably far closer to the real New Testament meaning of the word.

3. Furthermore, we cannot even assume that each writer in the New Testament used any given word with exactly the same meaning. Words usually have several different shades of meaning. One writer may have used a word to communicate one thing while another used the same word to communicate a different concept. For example, in the Gospel of John, *flesh* is used to indicate the frailty and weakness of a human being, with no moral overtones or connotations. But Paul used the same term to refer to man's sinful condition.

4. We should not strive so hard to find the minute technical meanings of any particular word. The New Testament was written in the common, ordinary language of the man in the street. For its day, it was neither technical nor particularly pious. It was "people talk." We must be careful not to assume that words which had specifically technical meanings were always so used in the New Testament. Language which had a technical meaning for a priest in Jerusalem might not have carried such a meaning to the Christians at Corinth. God communicates his truth to people in language which they can understand. The army may describe a shovel as "a manual earth-moving instrument," but God doesn't.

5. Watch out for idioms. These can frequently be misleading to a contemporary interpreter. We must be aware that idiomatic expressions may convey a meaning far beyond, and possibly even different from, its literal meaning. The term *New Testament* is itself such an idiom. Taken literally, it would refer to a new will left by someone deceased. But due to its Old Testament usage in Jeremiah

31:31-34, the idea was used idiomatically in the New Testament to refer to the new relationship and commitments between God and his people.

It is only as we begin to understand clearly what the various words in a sentence mean and how they are related to one another that we shall be able really to interpret that sentence. However, there is yet one more process through which we must go in discovering what the New Testament writer was actually saying.

### Identify the Historical, Geographical, and Literary References

When trying to determine the meaning of any particular New Testament verse, we must identify any references which it may have to historical events, to geographical places, or to literary sources. Any of these latter may refer to something either within or without the Bible. For example, the New Testament makes frequent use of Old Testament quotations. In order to fully understand what the New Testament writer is talking about, we must go back and seek to understand what the Old Testament reference is saying. Furthermore, the New Testament also makes occasional references to quotations from Greek poets or to other extrabiblical Hebrew material. Learning the full meaning of those quotes in their original sources can be an aid to interpretation.

Geographical references should always be checked against a good biblical map. The experience of Paul's vision of the man from Macedonia takes on new meaning when the entire passage is read with good maps in hand (see Acts 16:6-10). When Paul and his party were journeying, every door of mission was closed to them until they got to Troas, where there was nothing but the sea in front of them. But, just as it appeared that every door was closed, God called them across the sea.

Historical references also add more meaning to your passage when you look them up and get the basic information. Paul's references to the patriarchs in Romans 9 give significant depth to the meaning of that passage when we understand those references.

We should not just assume that we know what is being referred to, we should actually look it up and study it. Furthermore, knowing the historical and cultural background of a city like Corinth adds greatly to our understanding of Paul's correspondence with the Christians of that city.

To find these references, the marginal notes of your Bible will be of help. Also, good commentaries can aid significantly. Furthermore, check the indexes of your historical and archeological books for references to the particular passage which you are studying. Finally, read the introductory material in your New Testament introduction which deals with the particular book you are studying.

## Summary

The entire procedure which has been discussed in this chapter has had one purpose: determining what any particular New Testament text says, after we have determined what words are really in the text. (Review the preceding chapter for this procedure.) The procedure which we have described in this chapter is the one which is usually most frightening to persons who wish to learn how to interpret the Bible with accuracy. Most of us are extremely insecure when it comes to English grammar. Don't let this fear turn you aside from your stated goal of becoming a good biblical interpreter. It is worth the effort of mastering.

In order to help you get a better grasp of the process, I will summarize the essential tasks in a step-by-step procedure. If you follow this, it will lead you to the goal of knowing what any New Testament text really says.

Step 1. *Consider the grammar and syntax.* Remember that both of these in the original Greek are far more similar to English than was the Hebrew of the Old Testament. Your own knowledge of English plus good commentaries will help you at this point. Be sure that you know exactly what the subject, verb (predicate), direct object, and indirect object are. You need to have a clear understanding of exactly how the sentence is put together. Everything else will likely be in error if you are in error here. Do not proceed beyond this point until you are clear in your own mind as to how the inspired author has put the sentence together.

*Step 2. Identify the kind(s) of action(s) set forth in your verse.* It is imperative that you know whether the action is past, present, or future. It is also necessary that you be able to distinguish between commands, simple statements, questions, wishes, suggestions, or desires. One major difference between Greek verbs and English verbs is the fact that verb forms usually indicate whether action is punctiliar, linear, or completed. Those who cannot read Greek can only find this out from a good commentary.

*Step 3. Consider the punctuation.* New Testament sentences often get quite involved. Therefore, in order to make sense out of them, the punctuation becomes vitally important. Make sure that your understanding of the grammar and syntax of a verse is communicated by its punctuation.

*Step 4. Consider word usages and their ancient meanings.* This focuses upon the way words and phrases in your sentence were used elsewhere in the New Testament and in the New Testament world. Identify idioms and figures of speech, and be sure that the related passages which you investigate actually used the same Greek expression. Considering identical English words which translate different Greek words will lead you astray. Avoid this pitfall by using your analytical concordance.

*Step 5. Consider contemporary word meanings.* It is imperative that you use contemporary words which communicate as nearly as possible what the ancient author was saying. Furthermore, your choice of a contemporary word will be dependent upon the audience to whom you are planning on teaching or speaking. For example, *grace* is a good New Testament word. In most situations, it is a good, communicating word to an adult church audience. But to most people in a non-Christian culture, it probably sounds more like a woman's name than anything else. You should do your best never to use a word which your audience will likely misunderstand.

*Step 6. Identify historical, geographical, or literary references.*

Until you are clear on these matters, there is always a real possibility that you may fail to really know what your text says.

## Practice Exercises

The same kind of warning which was issued for accomplishing this task with the Old Testament needs to be repeated here. With practice you will develop both skill and speed. However, you must never let your desire for speed get in the way of doing a good job. Accuracy is essential. Speed is not.

Furthermore, not every step will produce additional understanding. However, you cannot know this until you have done it. Do not skip anything if you do not know that it will be fruitless.

Finally, the exercises which I have selected will enable you to get some experience in dealing with this procedure. The questions which I ask will help you come to grips with each step of the procedure.

1. Matthew 28:19-20

(1) Who is the subject of the first part of the passage? Is the subject actually stated or is it merely understood?

(2) What kind of verbs are used in the first half of the passage? Check a good commentary or two before you answer this. Then identify each verb. Did any translation which you used indicate the kind(s) of action which the commentaries say is actually indicated here? How would you modify the translation in order to communicate the real action?

(3) In what way does the punctuation indicate that the verse has two major sections?

(4) Who or what is the subject of the last part of the passage?

(5) Who or what is the indirect object or beneficiary of the last part of the passage?

(6) In considering word usages, carefully consider each of the following: *disciples, all nations, baptizing,* the significance of *name, teaching, observe, always,* and *the close of the age.* Which are most significant?

(7) Which of these words could be better communicated to a contemporary church audience by using different words? What would you choose? What words would you choose if you were trying to say this same thing to a nonchurch audience?

(8) Are there any historical, geographical, or literary references which need to be identified?

(9) In the light of all of these elements, how would you state a tentative translation of this passage?

2. Acts 1:8

(1) How many clauses or separate statements does this passage have? What are they?

(2) In the first two clauses, identify the subject, the verb (the action), and the object of the action.

(3) In the last clause, who is the subject and what is the action?

(4) Particular study should be devoted to the following words: *power, Holy Spirit, witnesses,* and *the end of the earth.*

(5) What does the use of the word *when* indicate to you?

(6) Can you locate the geographical references? What is being communicated by these references?

(7) How would you modify your tentative translation to make it clearer to a church audience? To a nonchurch audience? To a group of nine- through eleven-year-old children?

3. Ephesians 2:14-16

With this exercise, I am not going to ask questions to guide you. Simply follow the steps as outlined in the text. However, I will warn you that there is a historical reference to a practice which was common in the Temple of Jerusalem in New Testament times. Understanding this reference makes all the difference in understanding the passage. You will need to check your commentaries carefully here.

After you have completed these exercises, then begin to select some passages at random and try the techniques as I have outlined them. It might be of some value to select a larger passage upon which to focus your attention. Follow with Colossians as suggested in chapter 7. As you practice the procedures and begin to develop your skills, you will begin to feel a confidence which can only come through practice and achievement. At that point, you will be ready to move on to the next step.

Sample Work Sheet
DETERMINING WHAT THE TEXT SAYS (NT)

Text: Book, chapter, and verses

1. Significant grammatical and syntactical characteristics, including kinds of actions and punctuation

2. Key words including significant background and specific usage

3. Significant historical, geographical, and literary references

4. Revised tentative translation (if necessary)

# Part 4
## Moving from Preparation
## to Interpretation

# 9

# Discovering What the Text Meant

Although the process of preparing to interpret an Old Testament text (part 2) and of preparing to interpret a New Testament text (part 3) were similar, there was enough difference to justify dealing with them separately. However, once we have gotten to the place of having determined what either a New Testament or an Old Testament text says, the process of interpretation is the same for either. Therefore, we no longer have to deal with each Testament separately.

As I have pointed out, the basic presupposition of biblical interpretation is that *God is a God of sense, not of nonsense.* By this, I mean that whatever God revealed through his ancient spokesmen must have made sense both to them and to their hearers. If it had not made sense to the speakers and authors, they would have questioned God until it did. If it had not made sense to the hearers, they would never have preserved these materials. The very fact that we have a Bible at all, from a human standpoint, is an indication that it made real sense to the people. It spoke to them where they were.

To illustrate, this in no way means that the Hebrews fully comprehended all of the revelation contained in the Old Testament. It is obvious that they did not. If they had, then they would have been ready for the ministry of Jesus. On the other hand, it does mean that what they understood of God's revelation to them had a sensible meaning for their time. The same can be said of the New Testament. Since any future meaning of a passage must spring from its initial meaning, it becomes imperative that we seek to come to grips with what the text actually meant when it was first spoken or written.

This brings us to the next step in our process of interpreting the Bible. We have determined a tentative text for the passage under study. Following this, we have sought to come to grips with what any text really says by studying its grammar, syntax, punctuation, and key words. Now we must seek to answer the question, "Based upon our study to this point, what did the text mean when it was first presented?" It is imperative that we answer this question to the best of our ability before we proceed further in our task of interpretation.

## Determine the Literary Category

The first step in the process of determining what a passage originally meant is the identification of its literary category. We must know whether it was prose or poetry before we can know what it meant. Generally, prose can be understood in a rather straightforward manner, while poetry requires a bit more thought for understanding. For example, it is quite tender for a young man to tell his girl friend, "You are my kitten." But she would be very insulted to hear him say, "You are a cat." Taken literally, both expressions say about the same thing. But the former statement is poetic, expressing feelings which lose a great deal when expressed in simple prose. Thus you need to remember that poetry is generally used to express emotions or concepts which are difficult to set forth in straightforward prose. Thus, to understand what a poetic statement meant, we must try to get into the heart and emotions of the author. We must try to feel what he felt. A great deal of the Old Testament is poetry, but very little of the New Testament is. However, some parts of the New Testament are quite poetic, even though they are not poetry. (Note the Beatitudes in Matt. 5, for example.)

However, we must also be aware that not all prose can be handled as a simple straightforward statement. For example, Jotham's fable in Judges 9:7-15 is prose, but it cannot be taken literally. He was not talking about trees and brambles, but about Abimelech and the kingship. Another kind of prose which cannot be taken at its face value is apocalyptic literature. The visionary language of Daniel and Revelation obviously has a meaning far beyond a simple straightforward understanding of great beasts with numerous horns and multiple heads. It becomes imperative to search for the meaning behind the symbols. In general, however, prose can be handled in a much more straightforward manner than poetry. The point is that before we can move on with our attempt to determine what a passage originally meant, we must carefully identify its literary characteristics and note how they influenced its meaning.

### Determine the Context in the Book

With very few exceptions, the Bible is not a collection of truisms, meaningful quotations, or simple statements of faith. Outside of the Book of Proverbs, some sections of Leviticus, and a few similar passages, biblical texts are parts of sermons, narratives, hymns, liturgies, letters, and historical records. As such, they are closely related to what precedes and what follows them. If we are going to deal adequately with the meaning of a text, we must consider the context in which it is found, the material around it in the book from which it comes.

Now this means that we must deal with the biblical context in significant detail. As important as it is, it is not enough just to have a general idea of the message, purpose, or theme of the book. Every interpreter should be able to express the basic message of any book in the Bible in a simple, clear statement. This should never be more involved than a paragraph. But to deal with a specific text, we need a much more detailed understanding of the contents of a book. What is needed at this point is at least a paragraph-by-paragraph content outline. It is even more preferable to have a verse-by-verse outline. But the question arises as to where and how we can get such an outline.

The first time you have a passage to interpret from any book in the Bible, you should refer to at least two good critical commentaries, looking for their detailed outlines of the book. (More than two may be used, but at this point too many commentaries can get in the way.) Comparing the outlines in the commentaries with a good modern-language translation of the book, prepare your own outline of the book. You might actually wind up copying one outline completely, but do so only after you have thoroughly compared the outlines with the biblical material itself.

It is obvious that such a process will be time-consuming. But when it is done, you will have your own outline of the book (or at least one with which you agree). This can be added to your notebook or files for further use. Over a period of time, you will compile a complete set of outlines of all the books of the Bible. It should also be noted that you may wish to alter or modify your outline over the years as you deal with other passages. *Never assume that you have arrived at the last word in outlining the content of any biblical book.*

Once you have a detailed outline of the contents of the book from which your text comes, then you are ready to carefully examine its context. Locating exactly where in the outline your passage occurs, consider the major heading under which it comes. Ask yourself the following questions:

1. How does my passage fit into this section? Is it the conclusion? The introduction? Or a part of the development?

2. What does my passage add to this section?

3. How do the verses immediately preceding it lead to my passage? Is it a theological development? A logical development? A chronological development? Or some other kind of relationship?

4. How do the verses immediately following my passage relate to it? What kind of development do they indicate?

5. Is the passage I am seeking to interpret of major or minor significance to the context?

6. Is my passage of major or minor significance to the overall development of the book? What does it add to the basic message or theme?

7. Why does it appear that this passage was placed here? (Obviously this can only be an educated guess.)

Only after you have answered these questions are you ready to move on to the next step in determining what your passage meant originally. Not every one of these questions will have an answer in every instance. But you dare not assume that there is no answer. Neither do you dare assume that the answers may not be important. The only way by which you can make that judgment is by evaluating your answers after you have gotten them.

## Discover the Historical Setting

The process of placing a passage in its context within the book may or may not have given you a particular point in time to which the passage was addressed. For example, consider interpreting Isaiah 6:8, "And I heard the voice of the Lord saying, 'Whom shall I send, and who will go for us?' Then I said, 'Here am I! Send me.'" The context in which it is found clearly dates it to a specific point in time, "the year that King Uzziah died" (Isa. 6:1). But even when you know that, do you actually know anything about the real historical context? It is highly probable that you do not.

At this point, then, you must seek to discover the actual historical setting of your passage. You need to try to find out what was going on in the world at that time. Particularly, you need to try to find out what was going on which might have influenced the speaker or writer, and the people around him. This can become rather involved, but is very necessary if we are going to find out what a passage really meant. Furthermore, you may discover that the historical background of words which were spoken or of the events which happened might have been different from the background when the words were written down. In other words, there may be, and frequently are, two relevant historical backgrounds. Not all material was actually written in the form in which we have it immediately after it happened or was spoken. For example, the events of the Book of Ruth are actually set in the period of the judges, from around 1200 BC to around 1030 BC. However, the book was probably written in the form in which we now have it sometime after the time of Ezra, many centuries later. It was at this time that the Hebrews were developing an extreme exclusivism with a desire to drive out all foreigners from their midst. At such a time, the book might have come with a reminder that even their greatest king, David, was the grandson of a foreigner. God had a concern for people other than Israel (Ruth 4:18-22). Thus both the historical background of the events and the historical background of the writing can become important in seeking to determine what a passage actually meant.

Step 1 in determining the historical background of a passage is the Bible itself. In many of the books, the date is indicated within your passage or in a nearby passage. You must carefully examine the passage and its context for every historical clue. However, all too often, the dates are given in such a way as to be meaningless to most of us. For example, "the year that King Uzziah died" of Isaiah 6:1 does not really tell us much. Neither does the statement, "In the days of Ahaz," from Isaiah 7:1. At this point, there are several additional steps which you will need to take in order to come to grips with the historical background of your passage.

Step 2 in the process is to take your analytical concordance and look up every passage which will shed additional light on the period under examination. In the two examples given above, you should check out every reference to Uzziah or to Ahaz. Further, in the case of the second passage (Isa. 7:1), you should follow up on references to the other kings mentioned. This will begin to give you a picture of the biblical evidence dealing with the appropriate historical background.

Step 3 in establishing the historical background will usually be to refer to a good Old Testament or New Testament history book. Look up the significant names in the index and read the relevant references. Also, check the historical tables which biblical history books usually have to ascertain the actual chronological framework. (You should be aware that history books may differ slightly in their reconstruction of such ancient history. Don't let this become a stumbling block to you. They are dealing with incomplete evidence and therefore minor differences should be expected.) Once you have determined an actual or approximate date in history for the passage which you are interpreting, read the relevant sections in your Old Testament history and in your archaeological references. Obviously, if you cannot determine such a date, you will have to skip this step.

Step 4 in determining the historical background of your passage is to refer to the commentaries which you are using. They will usually shed some light both as to the date of the events or words of the passage, as well as upon a suggested date of writing. Let me warn you at this point, read such comments with both an open mind and a critical judgment. Evaluate what is said and weigh it in your own thinking. If this step allows you to establish a specific date, then refer to the biblical histories and archaeological resources in order to broaden your knowledge of the historical background.

Step 5 in discovering the historical setting is to consolidate and organize the historical information you have gathered which relates to the text you are interpreting. Make a list which will include as much of the following as you have been able to find. As you add each item to the list, be sure to record the source from which you got the information (i.e., from the Bible, from a history book, from an archaeological resource, from a commentary, or from any other source which you might have used). This will enable you to recheck it later if you need to do so.

1. What was the approximate date of the event, sermon, and so forth, which you are interpreting?

2. What was going on among the specific audience at that time? For clarity, it may be necessary to divide these items into religious, political, social, economic, ethical, and miscellaneous events.

3. Which of these items appears to be significant for understanding the passage in question? Why do you think so? (Be sure that there is a good reason for either including or eliminating each item on your list.)

4. How do the items which you have decided are significant affect your understanding of what the passage meant?

5. If it can be determined, what do you think was the approximate date of writing the passage which you are studying? Why have you come to that conclusion?

6. What was going on among the specific audience at the approximate time of writing the passage? Again, categorizing these events will probably prove helpful.

7. Which of these events or items appear to be significant for interpreting the passage? Why?

8. How do these items affect your understanding of what the passage meant?

When you have dealt with these questions to the best of your ability, then you are ready to move on to the next step.

## Consider the Theological Context

No part of the Bible was written in a theological vacuum. Quite the contrary, it was the book of faith (Israel's faith in the Old Testament, the churches' faith in the New Testament). The Bible had a historic faith, with a historical development. Furthermore, the Old Testament is the foundation upon which Jesus built his ministry and from which the early Christians preached Jesus to their world. Therefore, the whole Bible is a theological book, which has a significant place in the development both of Israel's theology and of that of the followers of Jesus.

Thus, in seeking to understand what any passage meant, we must seek to place it in the context of a developing theology. To fail to do this is to stumble over a major step in interpretation. Let me warn you, this is not easy, but it must not be ignored. Far too often interpreters simply ignore this step.

A second warning needs also to be noted here: Not every passage has a major place in the developing theology or faith of the Bible. Do not try to make a passage theologically significant when it is of only minor importance to any theological development.

In seeking to place a passage in its theological context, there are several steps which you must follow. As we have seen before, the place to begin is with the Bible itself. Specifically, begin with the passage which you are trying to interpret. Read it carefully, making a note of any basic theological concept which you think is, or may be, reflected in it. Underline the portion of the verse which seems to relate to this concept. Consider the following examples. I have used bold type to indicate portions you might underline.

Example 1. Isaiah 6:6-8

> Then flew one of the seraphim to me, having in his hand a burning coal which he had taken with tongs from the altar. And he touched my mouth, and said: "Behold, this has touched your lips: *your guilt is taken away and your sin forgiven.*" (1) And I heard the voice of the Lord saying, *"Whom shall I send, and who will go for us?"* (2) Then I said, *"Here am I! Send me."* (3)
>
> (1)  The doctrine of forgiveness
> (2)  The doctrine of God's call
> (3)  The doctrine of missions
>
> (You might also wish to list the seraphim as a part of the doctrine of angelic beings.)

Example 2. Ecclesiastes 12:13

> The end of the matter; all has been heard. *Fear God, and keep his commandments;* (1) for this is the whole duty of man.
>
> (1)  The doctrine of man

Example 3. Galatians 4:4-7

> But when the time had fully come, *God sent forth his Son, born of woman,* (1) born under the law, *to redeem those who were under the law,* (2) so that we might receive *adoption as sons.* (3) And because you are sons, God has sent the Spirit of his Son into our hearts, crying, "Abba! Father!" So through God you are *no longer a slave but a son, and if a son then an heir.* (3)
>
> (1)  The doctrine of incarnation
> (2)  The doctrine of redemption

(3) The doctrine of sonship, or the family of God

Example 4.  Colossians 2:13-14

> And you, who were *dead in trespasses* (1) and the uncircumcision of your flesh, *God made alive together with him,* (2) having *forgiven us all our trespasses,* (3) having canceled the bond which stood against us with its legal demands; this he set aside, nailing it to the cross.

(1) The doctrine of sin
(2) The doctrine of salvation
(3) The doctrine of forgiveness

Once you have determined which, if any, basic theological concepts your passage proclaims, then you must consider what it adds to that doctrine, or how it alters it. At this point, it would be well to refer to a good theological dictionary. Remembering that the Old Testament covers such a long period of history, it should not be surprising that most of its teachings show some historical change. This is even true within the New Testament with its briefer historical span. Therefore you may occasionally find some help in your history resource as well. What you are seeking to determine are the answers to the following questions.

1. Does this passage add anything new to the biblical understanding of this doctrine? If so, what does it add?

2. If it does not add anything to the concept, does it clarify a point about which the biblical teachings might not have been so clear before? If so, what?

3. Is this passage used anywhere else in the Bible? (Your concordance will help you answer this.) How was it used in the other place(s)? Does it have the same or a different theological emphasis?

4. How does (do) the theological concept(s) set forth here change from the earliest Old Testament concept to the full New Testament proclamation?

One warning must be carefully noted: do not base any major teaching on just one passage. If it is of major importance, God deals with it over and over again. If your theology can be destroyed by someone cutting a page out of your Bible, your theology is probably shaky.

### Evaluate the Levels of Understanding

Most of us approach the Bible as if we were dealing with just one level of understanding. That is just not so. In the Old Testament itself, there are at least three levels of understanding. If we are going to have any grasp of what a passage meant, we must seek to identify these levels of understanding, separating them if possible.

First, there was the official approach to their faith. This was that which was held by the priests, and might be considered the stance of so-called organized religion. Second, there was the popular understanding, the approach to faith held by the man in the street. Third, there was the prophetic understanding which was generally held by the leading spokesmen for God. Amos 7:10-17 illustrates a time when the official understanding and the prophetic understanding were in conflict. We must note, however, that sometimes there was even a division between the prophets, when one prophet held to a viewpoint different from the basic "prophetic" approach. Jeremiah and Hananiah had a major conflict over just such a confrontation (Jer. 27:1 to 28:17). There Hananiah was supporting the popular understanding.

These various approaches to the faith of Israel were not always in conflict; sometimes they were in agreement. Generally, however, at least one of these levels of understanding differed from the others. Furthermore, just because there was a difference in some points did not mean that they differed at all points. Job's friends, for example, said many things which were correct. But they also said some things which were wrong. As representaives of popular religion, they at times agreed with the prophetic point of view and at times differed from it. But at the end, we are told: "The Lord said to Eliphaz the Temanite: 'My wrath is kindled against you and against your two friends; for you have not spoken of me what is right, as my servant Job has' " (Job 42:7).

The point of all this is that in dealing with any passage we must seek to disentangle these three levels of understanding. Is the text with which you are dealing a representative of the official viewpoint, the prophetic viewpoint, or the popular viewpoint? Or, is it a combination of one or more of these? Furthermore, if it does not represent all three points of view, is it in conflict with the one (or two) which it does not represent? While these questions are sometimes very difficult to answer with certainty, we must attempt an answer. In trying to find an answer to these questions, there is almost no help available outside of the biblical text itself. Thus, it is extremely important to read the larger passage around your text with great care and thought. Further, you must carefully compare your text and its theological insights with your knowledge of all of the rest of the Old Testament. Commentaries can be of some help here, but they do not offer a great deal of guidance.

In the New Testament, there are also multiple levels of understanding. First of all, there might have been a specific Old Testament teaching concerning a particular idea. In addition, there may also have been a common or official first-century Judaism approach to the same idea which might have been different from that of the Old Testament. Then, there may also have been a popular Christian view and even a heretical Christian view to a subject. Finally, there may also have been the teaching of Jesus or of his Spirit through the New Testament speakers or writers.

To illustrate these different concepts or levels of understanding, consider the question of sabbath observance (Mark 2:23-27). The Old Testament commanded sabbath observance (Ex. 20:8-11). But the Judaism of Jesus' day, under the influence of the Pharisees, had multiplied the laws concerning sabbath observance; so here is another level of understanding. Finally, there is the teaching of Jesus concerning the sabbath. In other places, we frequently find the teachings of Jesus and the understanding of the disciples to be widely separated from another. It is important when interpreting any text to consider its particular level of understanding. It is only as you identify the appropriate levels of understanding that you will really be able to discover what the text meant in its day.

When you have completed your analysis of the level(s) of understanding reflected in your text, write down the level(s) of understanding you find there and give the reasons for your answer. Be sure that the reasons you list really support the answer you gave.

## Draw Your Conclusions

All of the material in this chapter has been aimed at helping you to determine exactly what the text meant when it was spoken and/or written. If you do not decide this, then you will have wasted your effort. In helping you to do this, we need to review what we have done. If you have done everything properly, you should now have answers to all of these questions:

1. How does this passage fit into its book?
2. What does this passage add to its book?
3. What kinds of development flow through this passage?
4. How important is this passage to the book and its message?
5. What is the historical period in which the passage occurred or was spoken? When was it apparently written down?
6. What of significance was going on in the biblical world at the time the passage occurred or was spoken? What was going on when it was written?
7. How do these items affect our understanding of the passage?
8. What major doctrines, if any, are taught in this passage?
9. What new thought or development did this passage add to their theological understanding?
10. What part of their theological understanding was clarified by this passage?
11. What level of theological understanding does this passage reflect?

When you have answers to all of these questions, you will then be in a position to attempt an answer to our major question: *What did the text mean when it was first presented, either in action, in spoken word, or in writing?* Write your answer down so that you can properly analyze it. When you have answered this question, look back over your answers to the preliminary questions. Be sure that your answer to the main question is in line with everything you have discovered about the text thus far. If it is not, then you need to revise it.

The major warning at this point is to *be sure that you allow your answer to grow out of your study.* Do not try to force your preconceived notions upon it. For those of us who have done much preaching or Bible teaching, this may be difficult. Once we have previously interpreted a passage, it might be difficult to admit that we may have been wrong about it. But if we fail to admit that we might have been in error, then we are neither in a position for God's Spirit to lead us into new truth (John 16:12-13) nor are we in a position to be forgiven for our past sins of poor interpretation. If we sin in other areas of our lives, let us not deceive ourselves into thinking that we have not failed here as well.

## Summary

To this point, you have moved through three major steps in interpreting any biblical passage. First, you should have arrived at a tentative translation of your text. Second, you have made a study of what the text says. This should have given you a list of significant items of grammar and/or syntax, as well as a list of major words and their meanings. Third, you have now determined, in the light of the above, what the text actually meant when it was first spoken or written. You should have a simple statement or paragraph to set forth your conclusion. It may be that at this point you will need to go back and revise your tentative translation. You should consider whether or not this is necessary. From this point on, your text is no longer tentative but fixed. Nothing else which you do should alter it.

## Practice Exercises

As in other steps, the only way to develop any skill in this process is to practice, practice, and then practice some more. Practice will help you both to lose your fear of the process as well as to develop confidence in applying it. The exercises which follow have been selected to help you at this point. Further, in order to simplify your having to locate a passage in the context of its book and to make it easier in mastering a historical background, we will confine all future Old Testament exercises to the Book of Amos, and all future New Testament exercises to the Epistle to the Colossians. Therefore, before actually giving the exercises, I am giving a content outline of both Amos and Colossians.

OUTLINE OF THE BOOK OF AMOS

I.  The book of sermons (1:1 to 6:14)
    A. Setting of the ministry (1:1-2)
       1. Historical background (1:1)
       2. Major theme (1:2)
    B. Judgment on the nations (1:3 to 2:16)
       1. Foreign nations condemned for inhumanity (1:3 to 2:3)
          a. Syria accused of extreme cruelty (1:3-5)
          b. Philistia accused of treachery (1:6-8)
          c. Phoenicia accused of betrayal (1:9-10)
          d. Edom accused of perpetual hatred (1:11-12)
          e. Ammon accused of inhumane greed (1:13-15)
          f. Moab accused of desecration of the dead (2:1-3)
       2. Judah condemned for rejecting God's law (2:4-5)
       3. Israel condemned for rejecting God's love (2:6-16)
          a. Injustice and idolatry (2:6-8)
          b. The loving blessings of God (2:9-11)
          c. God's blessings rejected (2:12)
          d. The coming judgment (2:13-16)
    C. Accusations against Israel (3:1 to 4:5)
       1. All Israel included (3:1)
       2. The peril of privilege (3:2)
       3. Basis for the prophet's attack (3:3-8)
          a. Questions with obvious answers (3:3-6)
          b. Warning through God's prophets (3:7-8)
       4. Foreigners called to execute judgment (3:9-11)
       5. The totality of destruction (3:12)

6. Judgment upon the uncaring wealthy (3:13 to 4:3)
   a. Symbols of wealth destroyed (3:13-15)
   b. Attack upon the luxurious women (4:1-3)
7. The emptiness of meaningless worship (4:4-5)
D. The redemptive nature of judgment (4:6-13)
   1. The failure of famine (4:6)
   2. The failure of drought (4:7-8)
   3. The failure of blight (4:9)
   4. The failure of pestilence (4:10)
   5. The failure of destruction (4:11)
   6. A final confrontation with God (4:12-13)
E. God's lament over Israel (5:1 to 6:14)
   1. Grief over destruction (5:1-3)
   2. God's invitation (5:4-9)
      a. The invitation to life (5:4-5)
      b. The invitation to avoid judgment (5:6-7)
      c. The Author of the invitation (5:8-9)
   3. The sins of Israel (5:10-13)
   4. The invitation repeated (5:14-17)
      a. Evidence of seeking God (5:14-15)
      b. Judgment for rejecting God (5:16-17)
   5. The inescapable day of the Lord (5:18-20)
   6. The true nature of worship (5:21-27)
      a. Empty worship rejected (5:21-23)
      b. Real worship in life (5:24)
      c. Punishment for false worship (5:25-27)
   7. Warnings of the coming judgment (6:1-14)
      a. Woe upon the comfortable (6:1-3)
      b. Woe upon the luxurious oppressors (6:4-7)
      c. God's hatred of the proud (6:8)
      d. Terrible results of judgment (6:9-10)
      e. The certainty of judgment (6:11-14)
II. The book of visions (7:1 to 9:15)
   A. The first vision: a plague of locusts (7:1-3)
   B. The second vision: a coming drought (7:4-6)

C. The third vision: God's measurement of Israel (7:7-9)
D. Interlude: Amos' vision of his task (7:10-17)
1. Amaziah, the priest of Bethel (7:10-13)
   a. The priest's report (7:10-11)
   b. The priest's attack (7:12-13)
2. Amos' report of his call (7:14-15)
3. Amos' message of judgment (7:16-17)
E. The fourth vision: the coming end (8:1-3)
F. Sermons upon the visions (8:4-14)
1. The audience characterized (8:4-6)
2. The certainty of judgment (8:7-8)
3. The consequences of judgment (8:9-14)
   a. Overwhelming grief (8:9-10)
   b. An absence of God's words (8:11-12)
   c. Death apart from God (8:13-14)
G. The final vision: God (9:1-15)
1. Inescapable destruction (9:1-4)
2. The majesty of God (9:5-6)
3. Privilege removed (9:7-8)
4. Israel scattered (9:9-10)
5. Hope beyond darkness (9:11-15)
   a. Blessings for the house of David (9:11-12)
   b. Restored fortunes for Israel (9:13-15)

OUTLINE OF THE EPISTLE TO THE COLOSSIANS

I. Salutation of the Epistle (1:1-2)
II. Prayers for the people (1:3-14)
A. Thanksgiving for the believers (1:3-8)
B. Prayers for their growth (1:9-14)
1. In the knowledge of his will (1:9)
2. In living a worthy life (1:10)
3. In strength (1:11-12)
4. A benediction of praise (1:13-14)
III. Theological concerns (1:15 to 3:4)
A. The supremacy of Christ (1:15 to 2:7)

    1. Supreme in the universe (1:15-20)
    2. Supreme in reconciliation (1:21-23)
    3. Supreme in Paul's ministry (1:24 to 2:5)
    4. Admonition to serve (2:6-7)
  B. The sufficiency of Christ (2:8 to 3:4)
    1. Sufficient over empty philosophies (2:8-15)
    2. Sufficient over false legalism (2:16-17)
    3. Sufficient over false worship (2:18-19)
    4. Sufficient over false asceticism (2:20-23)
    5. Sufficient over ultimate victory (3:1-4)
IV. Ethical admonitions (3:5 to 4:6)
  A. Transformation of belief and behavior (3:5-17)
    1. Giving up the old ways (3:5-11)
    2. Taking on the new ways (3:12-17)
  B. Admonitions concerning home relationships (3:18 to 4:1)
    1. Husband-wife relationships (3:18-19)
    2. Child-parent relationships (3:20-21)
    3. Slave-master relationships (3:22 to 4:1)
  C. A call to faithfulness (4:2-6)
    1. Faithfulness in prayer (4:2-4)
    2. Faithfulness in behavior (4:5-6)
V. Concluding words (4:7-18)
  A. Commendations and greetings (4:7-17)
  B. Benediction (4:18)

1. Amos 5:4-7

(1) What historical period is addressed by this passage? (See Amos 1:1; also check your Old Testament history of this period.)

(2) What kind of social and economic conditions characterized Israel during this time?

(3) What were the religious conditions in Israel?

(4) What is the significance of Bethel and Gilgal?

(5) What were the evidences that they had failed to seek God?

(6) What was to be the result of seeking God?

(7) What was to happen to them if they failed to accept the

invitation to seek God?

(8) How does this fit into the Book of Amos? What leads up to it? What does it lead up to?

## 2. Amos 8:11-12

(1) What is the historical background of significance for understanding this passage?

(2) How does this fit into the context of the book?

(3) Is this passage prose or poetry? What difference does it make in your understanding of it?

(4) What would you consider the theological context of this passage? Does it add anything to the development of that theological concept?

(5) What was this passage really saying to the people of Israel?

## 3. Colossians: 1:3-5a

(1) How does this passage fit into the context of the book?

(2) What do we learn of Paul's relationship to the Colossian church in this passage?

(3) How does this fit into your knowledge of the history of Christianity in Colossae?

(4) Was there anything going on in Colossae at this time which might have made this statement more significant? If so, what?

(5) What major doctrines, if any, are taught or clarified by this passage?

## 4. Colossians 2:6-7

(1) How does this passage fit into the context of the book?

(2) Does the contextual placing affect your understanding of this passage?

(3) What was the history of the Colossian church which might affect your understanding of this passage?

(4) What major doctrines, if any, are taught in this passage?

(5) How were the theological concepts of the Colossian church altered by Paul's teaching here?

## 5. Further suggestions

These examples will have shown you that not every question raised in this chapter is relevant to every passage which you undertake to interpret. With that understanding, now select several other passages from Amos and Colossians and try to determine what they really meant when they were initially proclaimed. Do this until you begin to feel familiar with the process and somewhat confident in its application.

When this step has been mastered, you are well on the way to being able to interpret any passage in the Bible. There is just one more major task which you must be able to do. We are now on the threshold of our ultimate goal.

Sample Work Sheet
DETERMINING WHAT THE TEXT MEANT

Text: Book, chapter, and verses

1. Literary category

2. Significance of the text's location in the book

3. Historical setting of the book

    A. Date

    B. Significant political factors

    C. Significant religious factors

    D. Significant social and economic factors

    E. Other significant factors

4. Basic theological teachings and their context

5. Basic levels of understanding reflected

6. What did the text really mean when it was spoken? Written?

7. Final Translation

# 10
# Determining What the Text Means

In general, most biblical interpreters fall into one of two pitfalls in relation to the step of determining what a text means. The first of these pitfalls is that of assuming that when you (or your audience) know what a passage meant originally, then anyone can apply it to contemporary life. Too many commentaries, too many Sunday School lessons, and too many sermons falter and fail at precisely this point. Determining what a passage meant originally and then just leaving it there is to fail God, yourself, and those to whom you minister.

Unfortunately, this is a game far too many Christians play. We like to talk about some other time, some other place, and some other people. But if the Bible is God's Word to us, then it has something to say to us here and now.

The second pitfall in trying to determine what the Bible means to us today is to assume that we can simply look at a text and immediately apply it to contemporary life, without relating its present meaning to its past one. That, too, is false. The nation of Israel was different from any modern nation. Their government was different; their economy was different; their social structures were different; and their religion was different. Furthermore, early Christianity was founded and grew in a world radically different from ours. Against this background, you and I as interpreters have the task of moving from the ancient meaning of a passage to its contemporary application. Since we are dealing with the same text, we cannot ignore its ancient meaning. To the contrary, its modern meaning should grow directly from its ancient meaning. Furthermore, just as

**183**

a translator is seeking to transfer a message from an ancient language into a modern one, so we as interpreters are seeking to translate an ancient meaning into a modern one. To fail at this point is to fail altogether.

To know what Isaiah and Amos or Jesus and Paul said to their people thousands of years ago may be of both religious and historical interest. But our task is to discover what God is saying to us here and now through those same men and their ancient words. There are four steps which lead to the accomplishment of this purpose.

## Analyze the Thrust or Movement of the Passage

### In the Old Testament

As we seek to determine what an Old Testament passage means, we need to remind ourselves that the Old Testament covered many centuries of God's dealing with his people Israel. It was not written all at one time, and it does not all deal with just one historical period. Therefore, we must recognize that the Old Testament presents its story against the background of Israel's belief that history was moving toward a goal. God was in control of history and it was ultimately moving toward his ends. Therefore we cannot deal with a particular passage as if it were a permanent bit of their philosophy or theology which was always true. In other words, any particular passage had in its background a set of beliefs which were being emphasized or modified as God continued to work with them in his plan of salvation.

As an example, consider the laws concerning Hebrew slaves.

> When you buy a Hebrew slave, he shall serve six years, and in the seventh he shall go out free, for nothing. If he comes in single, he shall go out single; if he comes in married, then his wife shall go out with him. . . .
> When a man sells his daughter as a slave, she shall not go out as the male slaves do. . . . And if he does not do these three things for her, she shall go out for nothing, without payment of money (Ex. 21:2-11).

In seeking to understand this passage, several factors stand out. To lift it up and seek to apply it literally today would be foolish, for the gospel of Christ has given us such a respect for the lives of others that slavery is totally impossible. On the other hand, can we just ignore this passage? If we believe that God preserved the Old Testament for us, then its presence there must have more than a historical interest. To properly understand it, we need to recognize the fact that all ancient societies, including Israel, practiced slavery in some form. Prior to this time in Israel, slaves were treated as nothing more than property. They could be bought and sold and were hardly even considered as people, let alone as citizens with rights and privileges under the law. Here, Israel was being told: "Slaves have rights, too." Thus, the passage was not merely regulating the treatment of slaves, it was moving in the direction of respect for persons, which would ultimately lead to the New Testament teachings of love for all people. Therefore, the passage has a *thrust* which we must grasp if we are going to properly apply it today.

*It is the task of the interpreter to determine the thrust of an Old Testament text.* We must know what went before and what the ultimate New Testament emphasis was. Then we can see how the passage we are studying carried its meaning forward.

This process of determining the thrust of an Old Testament passage was precisely the method which Jesus applied when he interpreted the Old Testament. When Jesus examined the Commandment, "You shall not kill," he indicated that the thrust or movement of the Commandment focused upon anger (Matt. 5:21; Ex. 20:13). The same kind of approach was made to the Commandment: "You shall not commit adultery" (Matt. 5:27; Ex. 20:14), where the thrust was seen to focus upon the inner attitude of lust. What he was saying was that when we control hatred in our hearts, there will be no killing with our hands. When we control lust within, there will be no outward adultery.

It is this determination of the thrust of a passage which helps keep the Old Testament in perspective. There have been countless interpreters who have stumbled over the famous (or infamous) law of retaliation (lex talionis), which says:

> You shall give life for life, eye for eye, tooth for tooth, hand for hand, foot for foot, burn for burn, wound for wound, stripe for stripe (Ex. 21:23b-25).

This falls far short of Jesus' teachings concerning turning the other cheek (Matt. 5:38-41). Of course it does. But, when we realize that in ancient Israel vengeance was the rule of the day, then we note that the thrust of this passage was saying that they could no longer demand or expect vengeance. Instead, they could claim nothing more than justice. In seeing this, we can then see the movement from vengeance to justice and ultimately from justice to mercy. Seen in such a light, this passage makes perfect sense. (It is probably worth noting that for many people in the world today, moving from a desire for vengeance to a simple claim for justice would be a major step forward along the pathway toward mercy.)

To determine the thrust or movement of a passage demands that you have done your work well up to this point. You must know what the passage under study really meant. Furthermore, you must have a clear understanding both of its Old Testament background and its New Testament implications. But please note, determining the thrust of a passage must not be mistaken for trying to make an Old Testament passage sound like the New Testament. It does not and, in general, it cannot. If the Old Testament had sounded like the New Testament, we would not have needed the New Testament.

### In the New Testament

It is usually easy for an interpreter to understand that Old Testament passages have a thrust, for it clearly was moving toward the New Testament. But we must now ask: Do New Testament passages have a thrust as well? Our immediate answer will probably be an unequivocal no. But before we settle upon that answer, let us at least consider the question more thoroughly.

To begin with, consider the words of Jesus to his disciples:

> I have yet many things to say to you, but you cannot bear them now. When the Spirit of truth comes, he will guide you into all the truth; . . . for he will take what is mine and declare it to you (John 16:12-14).

There is a forthright teaching here that God's Holy Spirit was going to guide the disciples into new truth, or additional truth, or into an enlarged understanding of the truth. This would at least indicate the possibility that by determining, under God's leadership, the thrust of a New Testament passage, we are opening our minds and hearts to God's leadership in fulfilling that of which Jesus spoke.

But we can go beyond this. Consider for a moment, Paul's Epistle to Philemon. The entire Epistle has to do with the relationship between a slave, Onesimus, and his master, Philemon. Does this mean that modern Christians should go back into the slave business? Of course not. Even though neither the Epistle to Philemon nor any other passage of the New Testament condemns slavery, there are countless passages on love which, if followed to their ultimate conclusion, make slavery absolutely impossible for a Christian to participate in. Here again, it is obvious that the thrust of ancient New Testament passages have led us to a teaching far beyond the actual words which were spoken or written then.

But beyond these ideas, the very nature of the churches' preaching ministries is based upon the assumption that the message of the New Testament must be carried forward in time and applied to our lives in this world. Even when a passage appears to be directly applicable to our day, we still are involved in trying to determine how our society has changed and, therefore, how the old story can meet the needs of a new society. So while a passage itself may not have an enlarged meaning, the very changes in the world have given the passage a thrust, a direction of movement.

Once you have determined the thrust or movement of any biblical passage, then you are ready to move on to the second step in seeking to determine what your text means. Knowing the thrust is important, but it is still just a step in the process.

### Determine the Central Truth or Principle of the Passage

The central truth or main principle of a passage is a single, simple statement of what the passage is about. It should be stated in the present or future tense to make sure that you are directing it to your intended audience. For example, "God gave the Ten Commandments to Israel" is not a good central truth for Exodus 20:1-17. It is certainly true, but a statement such as the following is much more relevant and applicable to a contemporary audience: "God gives commands to people in order to govern our relationships with him and with one another."

A good central truth should also be stated in the active rather than the passive voice. In the above illustration, it is much better to say, "God gives . . ." rather than to say, "Commandments were given by God. . . ." The Bible is a book of action. The Commandments both demand and expect action. Thus, to state a central truth in any way other than the active voice is to miss an emphasis of major significance.

In order to write a good central truth, it will be necessary to do it over and over again. Having done all of the steps to this point, ask yourself, "What is this passage really saying to me? What is it saying to those to whom I minister?" Write the answer down in one sentence. Then test it with these questions.

1. Is my statement of the central truth simple? If it is not, rework it. The Old Testament always speaks in simple sentences. You should let it speak to you in the same way. While the New Testament sometimes uses quite involved sentences, its message is generally easily simplified. This certainly helps in understanding.

2. Is my statement of the central truth in the present or future tense? The present tense is usually preferable, for even when the prophets spoke to the future, they began with their present audience. If your central truth fails at this point, rewrite it.

3. Is my statement of the central truth in the active voice? If your statement is passive, rewrite it. God seems generally to have dealt with his people through verbs of action. Verbs which are passive seldom require anything of the hearer. But, as we have noted, both

the Old and the New Testaments demand response. Let us keep our central truths aimed in that direction.

4. Does my statement of the central truth spring from what the passage originally meant? If it does not, rewrite it. A contemporary central truth is the flower of the original root. Otherwise, you can make a passage mean almost anything you wish it to. If you can do this, so can everyone else and the result is that the passage has no meaning at all, at least it has no real meaning. But we all agree that this is false, so the error must be in our approach to the central truth. Keep your central truth growing out of the original meaning of the passage.

5. Is my statement of the central truth really what the passage is saying? If it is not, then you must rewrite it. It matters not how good a statement of theology or philosophy you may have; if it does not come from your passage, forget it. Far too many interpreters come up with a good, theologically true statement, and then try to force it upon the passage at hand. Do not be guilty of abusing the Bible like this. If you are starting with a text, let the text speak. Do not force your own ideas upon it. Do not use your text as a pretext.

Writing central truths sounds easy. In practice, it usually becomes the most difficult part of the process of interpretation. More interpreters fail here than on any other single step in the process of interpretation. You will discover that arriving at a good statement of the central truth of a passage requires writing, rewriting, and rewriting again. The best advice I can offer here is to be diligent and consistent. Do not give up over your first failures. Practice will surely help, but good central truths will never come either easily or simply.

## Consider Similar or Related Contemporary Situations

Once you have arrived at a good statement of the central truth, you are ready to begin moving toward applying that truth to a life situation. Your ability at this point will start with the broadness of your experience of life.

The question immediately arises as to how you can develop this kind of broad-based life experience upon which to draw. It obviously comes from a number of different areas. First, and most obvious, your knowledge of life in general depends upon your own personal experiences. Your real knowledge here depends both upon what has happened to you and what kind of thinking you have devoted to those experiences. Many of us learn little from what we have experienced, because we never stop to reflect upon it, to relate it either to our previous experiences or to others' experiences, nor to ponder its lessons. Experience may be the best teacher, but it has taught us nothing if we fail to learn the lesson.

The second area from which we draw our knowledge of life is from our friends and family. Here, you have seen others face many of the trials and experiences which are common to all people. What have you learned from their experiences? Again, what is of major importance is not merely what you have seen happen to them, but what you have learned from those experiences. You must be a serious student of life if you are going to be able to apply the truths of the Bible to life.

The third area from which we may draw a knowledge of life is from counseling and pastoral ministries. Now it may sound as if this is specifically related to preachers. That is not so. Any Christian has numerous opportunities both to minister to people pastorally and to share in their problems through some kind of informal counseling. The pastor may have more exposure in these areas, but he has no exclusive hold on the territory. Again, the amount you will have learned about life from such experiences really depends upon the kind of thought you have applied to it. Merely listening to someone's problems does not necessarily mean that you will have learned much about life from them.

A fourth area from which we may draw our knowledge of life is related to what we read, see, or hear. Here we must include newspapers, news magazines, TV (or radio) newscasts, magazines, books, and normal TV or radio programs. The regular survey of both world and local news will help you keep up with what is going on in the world. Best-selling books will help you keep abreast of what people are reading. (You should always be asking yourself, "Why are they reading such things?") Listening to popular music will help you know what people are thinking. Popular music becomes popular by expressing what people feel and think. Furthermore, listening to music does not make the demands upon their thinking that reading does, so it probably gets nearer to the real "gut-feeling level" of contemporary society.

Simply put, everything which happens to you or of which you know and everything which has happened around you goes together to become a part of your broad-based life experience. The value of these events and of this knowledge in interpreting the Bible will clearly depend upon the amount and quality of reflective thought which you have devoted to it. But it is all there, waiting to be drawn upon.

After you have arrived at a central truth for your passage, then ask yourself this question: What contemporary life situations or conditions do I know about which are similar to the one which originally gave rise to this passage? Or you might also ask: "To what life situations of which I know will this central truth apply?"

In answering these questions, be prepared to make a full list of the answers. Let your mind move freely over the full range of your background. After the list has been completed, then go back over it removing those things which are somewhat farfetched. You should not have to strain your imagination in order to justify a particular application. If you have to strain to justify an application, your potential audience will probably not be able to follow it at all.

There is so much difference between the government of ancient Israel and that of any modern nation as to make it virtually impossible to take a message given to a Hebrew king, for example, and apply it directly to an American President or an English Prime Minister. On the other hand, the crisis which Israel faced at any particular point in time might be similar to a national crisis which we face. Furthermore, it might also be similar to a personal or community crisis which some might be facing. Therefore, it is imperative that you do not just confine your thinking to a hunt for identical situations. You probably will not find them. It is similar situations for which you must be watchful.

After you have eliminated the more or less fanciful situations to which your passage might relate, your list should be pared to the very few potential applications which are most significant. (Should the Holy Spirit lead you to eliminate all potential applications, you should save this passage for another time.) At this point, you are now ready to specifically relate your passage to a contemporary life situation.

## Apply the Central Truth and the Thrust to a Modern Situation

In seeking to determine what the text really means, you have arrived at a basic thrust and a central truth for it. But this is still general. You have also arrived at a list of potential life situations to which the passage might be applied. The next question is, "How do you decide to which life situation(s) you are going to apply the passage?" You cannot leave your application general if you are going to let the Bible really speak through you to human need.

At this point, you must consider the potential audience for whom you are interpreting the passage. Begin visualizing faces and giving names to them. Consider their needs which are most pressing at the moment. If you are preparing a Sunday School lesson, think of the actual members of the class. What needs do they have because of their common age? What are their needs individually? Consider their families, their jobs, their friends, their spiritual needs, their emotional problems. In other words, make a spiritual inventory of the problems which your potential audience faces and the burdens which they bear. Note however, not all Scripture is problem oriented. You should also consider their joys, their victories, and the things which are making them happy.

The same sort of process should be carried out if you are preparing a sermon, except that here you would consider the needs of the potential congregation. Be realistic in assessing the needs. If you do not expect any lost people to be present at a specific service, do not list as a need "to place their faith in Jesus for salvation." Further, do not ignore the needs of any one group. If you regularly have a large number of children present, do not always focus on the needs of the adults only.

If you are preparing your Bible study for a group with which you are unfamiliar, try at least to visualize a group with which you are familiar which should be somewhat similar. In this way, your list of potential life situations which might be met will at least be realistic.

Once you have completed your list of potential needs for your expected audience, you should then organize the list with some degree of priorities. How widespread is a particular need? If it is faced by only one person, it is probably best to eliminate it. In a church which I pastored while I was in seminary, there was a lady who was a gossip. As soon as I arrived in town on the weekend, she was on the telephone, sharing with me all of the "dirt" which had happened while I was away. Finally, I got fed up with it and prepared a sermon just for her. I thought it was well done, and was really looking forward to the Sunday when I would preach it. Unfortunately, only one thing went wrong. When I walked into the pulpit that Sunday, the lady was not there. I could only hope that there was someone else there whom that sermon might have helped. I later promised my Lord that if I ever again had a sermon for just one person, I would deliver it privately.

When you have gotten your list of audience needs organized, then it should be compared with your earlier list of situations which your passage might address. Any need or situation which does not appear on both lists must be eliminated. By this process of checking and cross-checking, you will arrive at a few needs which your people have and which your passage addresses. If there are more than a few, then you should focus upon the most pressing and prevalent ones. It is at this point that you are really face-to-face with what your passage means to your audience right here and now. At this point you are ready to begin specifically preparing your sermon, devotion, or Bible study.

## Practice Exercises

In developing the skills necessary for determining what a text means for a contemporary audience, there are four types of practice exercises necessary. You will need to work on each of these areas in your personal study.

1. Determining the Thrust

### Amos 5:18-20

(1) In what ways does the passage indicate that the people of Israel were looking forward to the day of the Lord?

(2) What was the apparent popular view of the day of the Lord in Amos' day? Why do you think so?

(3) Checking with your concordance, your theological dictionary, and your commentaries, what was the view of the day of the Lord by the time of Jeremiah or Zephaniah? (Particularly note Zeph. 1:7-16.)

(4) What is the thrust or movement in Amos' view of the day of the Lord?

### Amos 5:21-24

(1) By referring to your Old Testament history and to your commentaries, discover what the popular concept of the sacrificial system was in Amos' time.

(2) Turning your thoughts to the New Testament, what ultimately happened to the sacrificial system insofar as Christians were concerned?

(3) In the light of your answers to the above, what was the basic thrust of Amos' message concerning the sacrificial system? Be careful that you do not put more into his mouth than was actually there.

### Colossians 3:22 to 4:1

(1) What was the cultural background behind this passage?

(2) Using your analytical concordance, see what other Old and New Testament backgrounds you can find for understanding these

verses. How do these affect your understanding of the thrust of the passage?

2. Deciding upon the Central Truth

### Amos 5:18-20

(1) In the light of the above exercise to determine the thrust of this passage, state the central truth for it.

(2) When you have completed it, ask these questions of it:

Is it simple?

Is it in the present or the future tense?

Is it in the active voice?

Is it related to what the passage meant when Amos first spoke?

Is it really what the passage is saying?

If you cannot answer each of these questions with an unqualified yes, then rewrite the central truth and try again.

### Amos 3:7-8

Do the same thing with this passage that you did for the preceding one. Keep working at it until you get a statement with which you are completely satisfied.

### Colossians 3:22 to 4:1

Follow the same procedure here as you did for the two preceding ones. You may find this the most difficult one of all for which to state a central truth. Keep working at it until you are satisfied that you have done the best you can.

3. Identifying Related Contemporary Situations

### Amos 5:18-20

In the light of your study of this passage and of your statement of its central truth, make a list of possible contemporary situations to which it might apply. Consider personal situations, political situations, and religious situations. Consider both local church conditions as well as denominational situations. Let your mind freely rove over any area of potential application as you make your list. When you have listed as many possible applications as you can identify, then go back and eliminate those which require a major stretch of the imagination. Where it is appropriate, collect similar situations together under one heading.

Amos 5:21-24; Colossians 3:22 to 4:1

Do the same things for these passages which you did for the preceding one.

## 4. Applying the Passage to a Modern Situation

Identify your audience's needs. Begin by visualizing the class or congregation to which you minister. If you do not have a specific ministry situation, then visualize one with which you are familiar. You might wish to consider the class or the church of which you are a member. Then start listing the particular needs of the people whom you have visualized. You may wish to gather these under the following headings:

Needs related to age group

Needs related to family

Needs related to work

Needs related to community

Individual needs: spiritual, economic, social, and so forth

Compare the needs with the potential situations. When the list is completed, then compare it with the contemporary life situations to which your passage might apply, as listed in the preceding exercise. Eliminate those items which are not found on both lists. When you have done this, then you will have a list of needs in your audience to which your passage may be applied.

Now you have moved from a biblical text to an interpretation which specifically applies to the people to whom you minister. The basic task of interpretation is done. It has not been easy, but it has been worthwhile, for now you can apply your passage to the lives of your people with confidence. God has a message for your people and he is using you as the instrument of communicating it. There is no more precious privilege than this.

Sample Work Sheet
DETERMINING WHAT THE TEXT MEANS

Text: Book, chapter, verses

1. State the thrust or movement (if any).

2. State the central truth.

3. List similar contemporary situations to that of the passage.

4. List actual audience needs.

5. List items found in both 3 and 4.

6. Relate central truth and thrust to items in 5.

# Part 5
# Moving from Interpretation
# to Presentation

# 11

# Developing a Sermon, Devotional Message, or Lesson Plan

Basically, we have accomplished that for which we originally set out. We have identified and outlined a simple, step-by-step method for developing the skills necessary to be able to interpret any passage of the Bible. In so doing, I have focused attention upon the methods and techniques which you will need to apply every time you approach the task. As I noted at the beginning, I have assumed that you will pursue the entire task in prayer, asking God's guidance. It is his Word which you are interpreting. To seek to do so without the leadership of his Holy Spirit is pure folly. Therefore, even though I have not made constant reference to prayer and to his leadership, I have assumed both.

The necessity for God's leadership in interpretation was a lesson which was taught to me both by precept and example by those professors who first guided me in the study of the Bible. On one occasion, one of my professors had assigned me a particularly difficult passage to translate and interpret. I had done the best job which I could in translating it. I had labored with my Hebrew text, the lexicons, the commentaries, and such similar tools. Yet I still was not clear as to what the passage meant. I went to my professor and told him of all my labors and of my frustration at failing to achieve a satisfactory result. When he had questioned me concerning all my labors, he simply said, "Well, let's pray together, asking God to guide us in understanding this passage." So we prayed together, and I went back to my studies. As I approached the process again, under God's leadership, things began to fall into place which I had not seen before. The Holy Spirit did not just drop the answer into my lap, but he did so guide my studies that the interpretation which had eluded me slowly became clear. He will continue to fulfill this ministry of guiding us into his truth.

But it is obvious that we are not merely seekers after the truth simply to know the truth. As interpreters of the Bible, it is our task to communicate that interpretation to people. This chapter is about the business of communication: preparing a sermon, devotional message, or Sunday School lesson to be presented to an audience.

Let me warn you, I am not really seeking to tell you how to do this in one chapter. For a detailed approach to these subjects, there are numerous, more exhaustive books to which you can refer. On the other hand, there are some basic principles regarding this process which can be shared here as hints toward fulfilling the ultimate process. It is these principles to which I wish to call your attention. The best, most accurate interpretation in the world will be of no value if you cannot or do not communicate it well. It is to that end that I offer these hints which have been gleaned from a lifetime devoted to communicating God's truths from his Word.

Although there is a decided difference between an hour devoted to Bible teaching, thirty minutes devoted to a sermon, or five minutes given over to a devotional, the same basic principles apply. It is only the ultimate developments and methods of presentation which will differ. It appears to me that there are five basic steps which must be followed by any interpreter who is trying to communicate the interpretation of God's Word. These must be mastered no less well than all which has preceded.

### Identify the Goal Expected or the Response Desired

If you aim at nothing, you will most certainly hit it. Having an aim, a goal, or a purpose for your message will not guarantee that you will accomplish it. Failing to have one will guarantee that you will accomplish nothing. It is imperative that you have a very clear idea of what you wish to accomplish with your message.

However, knowing that you should have a goal and having a good goal are two totally different matters. For a message communicating the Christian gospel, there are certain characteristics which a good aim should have. A good communicator will note these very carefully.

First, a good aim should be *person centered*. Too frequently we are more concerned with "covering the material" than we are in making some change in the people to whom we minister. How sad! Our aim should always be that those who hear us will respond. We should never just aim to cover a certain number of verses or to present our "three points and a poem." Rather, we should intend that our people will learn something from our material and/or be motivated to make some response to it.

Second, a good aim should generally be *action oriented*. In general, both the Old and the New Testament demand a response. Occasionally, a knowledge aim will be adequate. But knowledge alone is seldom a sufficient goal. You may have to communicate knowledge this time in order to set the stage for some kind of action response at a later time. However, it is far more preferable to impart knowledge and move on to the action aim in the same message or lesson.

Third, a good aim should be *realistic*. In other words, it should be achievable. We all have the aim to lead the whole world to Jesus Christ as Lord. But realistically, we never expect to achieve that with a single message. It is probably unrealistic to expect that every lost person present will respond to Jesus in any particular lesson. It is probably unrealistic to expect everyone present at any service to make some sort of positive response. At the same time, you should not set your goals so low that they present no challenge.

Fourth, a good aim should be *specific*. It should seek to meet one or more of the needs identified in chapter 10. If you want your audience to respond, what do you want them to do? If you do not know very clearly what you are trying to lead your people to do, you will never be able to communicate it to them.

Fifth, a good aim should generally be *measurable*. If you cannot measure the results, how will you know whether or not you have achieved the goal? We who communicate the good news are frequently deceived into believing all the compliments people give us about our messages. First of all, this will not do, because talk is cheap. It is easy to tell someone what a good job they are doing. Second, just because someone does not come up and tell you that what you just communicated was a lousy sermon or a poor lesson does not mean either that they did not think so or that it was not lousy.

Not every sermon or lesson will have measurable results. Further, many results will never be known until the judgment. At the same time, some results should be visible and should be expected to be so. A good aim will look for these.

Finally, a good aim will be *brief enough to be remembered.* If your aim is not brief enough to be remembered, the chances are that under the pressure of your presentation, you will forget it. It does not matter how good your aim is, if you leave it in your study it is little better than no aim at all. It is not necessary to tell your audience what your aim is. In fact, it is probably better if you do not. But *you must not forget it.* If you keep your aim clearly before you, then your whole presentation will be held together by it.

## Consider a Logical Development from Text to Response

More often than not, the text itself will furnish an outline for your presentation. This may be more true for a Sunday School lesson than for a sermon, and it may also be more true for a sermon than a devotional message. But even if the text doesn't furnish the outline, your development of the presentation should clearly move from the text to the response which you are expecting.

Occasionally we get so excited over some particular idea that we try to work it into every message or lesson we present. Don't let pet ideas intrude into your presentation. A certain preacher got so wrapped up in the importance of baptism that he devoted almost every sermon to it. The deacons of his church, trying to alleviate the situation, asked him if he would preach on the text, "But the Lord God called to the man, and said to him, 'Where are you?'" (Gen. 3:9). On the following Sunday, he read his text, and then said, "Now this text naturally divides itself into three points: First, Adam had to be someplace; second, God wanted to know where he was; and third, he needed to be baptized." This kind of presentation must be avoided at all costs. It looks ridiculous when put down on paper. Unfortunately, many of us have been guilty at some time or another of doing just this sort of thing.

The arrangement of your presentation should be so logical that anyone in your audience could easily follow it and could just as easily reconstruct it for someone else. The response you anticipate should logically flow from the passage you are interpreting. Many messages shift so radically from the scriptural content to the anticipated response that no one knows how the speaker got there. This must not be. Good communication must be able to be followed and clearly understood by your audience.

There are no set number of points to have in a presentation, but here (as elsewhere) a good rule to follow is: *Keep it simple.* If you get too many points in your presentation, it will be difficult to follow. Once you have done all of your study and learned so much, it is a real temptation to share it all at once. Resist that temptation! Share only what is germane to your presentation. Put the rest away and save it for some other time.

## Identify Appropriate Illustrations

The art of illustrating your presentation is technically not a part of biblical interpretation. Nevertheless, it is of such significance that at least a few words need to be said. First of all, a good illustration should do just what the name implies—shed light on the point you are trying to make. Again, we are frequently guilty of finding a good illustration and then stretching our lesson plan or sermon outline all over the place in order to use the illustration. If it does not really fit your particular presentation, save it for some other time.

Second, good illustrations should relate to life so that your hearers can identify with them. Therefore, you should use illustrations which are understandable to your audience. If your illustration needs to be explained, it is a poor illustration. The purpose of an illustration is to clarify, to make something clear.

Third, illustrations should be believable. Your illustration may be completely true, but if it is difficult to believe, you may lose the attention of your audience and bring your entire message into question. Do not use illustrations which will stretch the credulity of your hearers.

Fourth, illustrations should come from your personal experience or your reading. If you use an illustration which you have read, be sure that you give proper credit. Above all, do not tell something which happened to someone else as if it had happened to you. Such misrepresentation is simple lying. The presentation of the gospel should not be handicapped by the falsehoods of the one presenting it.

Fifth, you should seldom (preferrably, never) use illustrations drawn from books of illustrations. Such illustrations are used by too many people and therefore become too trite to illustrate anything clearly. It is better to have no illustrations than to use those which call attention to themselves or which bore the audience because of their familiarity.

Sixth, it is not necessary to illustrate every point. But if you need an illustration and do not have one, turn to the Bible for it. Good biblical illustrations relate to life, will increase the biblical knowledge of your people, and help to communicate the interrelatedness of the biblical truths.

Seventh, do not be guilty of getting your illustrations out of balance. It is probably better not ever to have more than two illustrations with any one point. But to have two or three with one point and none with the next can create a distracting element in your presentation. Do not be guilty of letting your people leave remembering your illustrations rather than the biblical message.

Eighth, illustrations may be entertaining, but should not be aimed at being entertainment. You are trying to communicate the biblical revelation, not show how good you are at telling jokes. If you are going to tell a humorous illustration, draw it from your own experience if possible. If you are going to tell a joke, do not use one that everyone has heard. In this day and age, almost everyone reads the *Reader's Digest.* Therefore, its jokes might get in the way because of their very familiarity. If a joke is to be an illustration, your audience should not know the punch line before you get there.

Ninth, when you draw an illustration from your own experience, be sure that you are not revealing from the pulpit or the lectern what has been shared with you in confidence. Also, you should never be insulting. Do not tell stories which will hold anyone up to ridicule. This was not Jesus' way, and it should not be ours. Do not hold racial groups or any other category of people up to ridicule. If you are going to attack someone, do it directly, not by innuendo. Jesus attacked the loveless self-righteousness of the Pharisees, but he never ridiculed them. Neither should we.

Tenth, good illustrations can be collected over a period of time. Note brief quotes or poems from your reading by writing them down on note cards. (I would suggest $3 \times 5$ cards due to their ease in handling.) Also, events which have happened to you can be noted on the same types of cards. Keep these in a file for use as needed. Be sure that you keep good records of where you use each illustration. That way you will not be guilty of using the same illustration twice before the same audience. If for some particular reason, it becomes necessary to use the same illustration twice with the same people, tell them that you are repeating it. That is far better than having them think you are doing it ignorantly or are presuming upon their ignorance in having forgotten it.

### Carefully Prepare the Introduction and the Conclusion

Your entire presentation should be well thought out and prepared. But your introduction and your conclusion normally should be written out in full. This does not mean that you should read them. However, these are probably the two most important parts of your message and should be most fully prepared.

Your introduction must grab the attention of your audience and make them want to hear all of the rest of your message. A good introduction should start right where your people are. It should be life centered, striking, and attention getting. If you do not make your hearers want to hear your message, there are countless other things which will draw their attention away so that they may never hear anything else which you say. If you have their attention from the beginning, the chances are that you can keep the attention of most of them. If you lose their attention in the beginning, you will probably never get it again.

On the other hand, the conclusion is equally as important since that is where you should nail down what you have been trying to accomplish throughout the entire presentation. Far too many of us have a good beginning and do a reasonably good job of presenting our material only to fizzle out at the end. It is sort of like dropping an ice-cream cone on a hot sidewalk. All you can do is just stand there and watch it melt. You can lay the foundation for a skyscraper and gather the materials adequate to build it to the heavens, but if all you do is erect a chicken coop, you have wasted your people's time and God's time. Make sure that your conclusion draws everything up to the demanding of a response. At the end of your presentation, your audience should be asking what you want them to do. Tell them. In clear, simple language, draw it all together, setting forth the response which you expect. Do not ever let your audience leave wondering what you really wanted of them. Your presentation should have, must have, a "so what?"

Sample Work Sheet

DEVELOPING A SERMON, DEVOTIONAL MESSAGE, OR LESSON PLAN

Text: Book, chapter, verses

1. State the goal or response expected.

2. Outline the development from text to response.

3. List illustrations for each major point of the outline.

4. Write out the introduction and the conclusion.

# 12
# Warnings and Advice

In covering the material set forth in the preceding chapters, there have been numerous warnings which I have made and repeated. In addition, as you really begin the task of interpreting the Bible, there are some words of advice which I would like to share. Therefore, I have collected both the warnings and the advice in this final section.

You are ready to begin what has become to me one of the most exciting tasks God has given me: the task of interpreting the Bible for God's people. It is exciting because the Bible is so rich and is filled with his truth. It is also exciting because from its study will spring unbelievable new insights into God's redemptive ministry from the earliest days of Israel through the ministry of Jesus and the mission and message of the early Christians. Finally, interpreting the Bible is exciting because it has so often been done poorly, or simply not been done at all. The opportunity of doing it well, of mining new truths from God's Word, will bring a fulfillment to your ministry to God's people. With that as background, now let me share these words of warning and advice.

## Do Not Expect It to Be Easy

On several occasions I have warned you that the task of intepreting the Bible is not easy. If it were, you would not have read this book in the first place. It is worth remembering that God has not called us to an easy way. The way of Christ is never easy.

At the same time, hearing the voice of God as he speaks through this ancient collection of books is worth the effort. Suddenly you will discover that Abraham, Isaac, Jacob, Moses, Samuel, David, Elijah,

**211**

Amos, Peter, Paul, Barnabas, and all those ancient saints become real people, living in situations remarkably like ours, facing crises strikingly like those we face. As God spoke to them, so we hear him speaking to us. As God used them, so we can see how he can use us. When words that have been meaningless take on meaning, we know that the efforts we have made, the energy we have expended, and the time we have utilized have all been worthwhile.

As we approach the Bible, our attitude must be that of the boy Samuel, when he said, "Speak, Lord, for thy servant is listening" (1 Sam. 3:10, author's translation). The labor of hearing the voice of God as he speaks over these centuries and across the culture gaps suddenly fades into insignificance in the light of actually hearing God's voice. You must not expect it to be easy. But neither must you expect it to be unrewarding.

## Do Not Expect It to Be Simple

Furthermore, as you seek to interpret the Bible, you must not expect the process to be simple. There are so many things which you must consider and so many details which you must master. Among the many things which must be mastered are history, geography, archaeology, and culture. You must master language characteristics, your own and those of the Old and the New Testaments. It will at first appear that you can never keep all of it straight. The task will appear to be quite complex at the beginning.

That is the very reason for knowing and following a step-by-step approach to the task. This can never make it simple, but it will keep the process orderly. In other words, if you start out without a procedure to follow, the task will become so complex that you will almost certainly drop the ball somewhere. Without a detailed procedure, there will be something which you will overlook or omit which may make your interpretation invalid.

As long as you follow the process, each individual step will be fairly simple. Even though not every step will produce results with every passage, the very time when you omit a step might be the time when that specific one would have produced a fruitful insight into the message of a particular passage. In chemistry, there is a precise procedure for taking any metallic substance and analyzing it to determine all of the various metals which are present. The process is long and laborious. But when it is followed precisely, the desired results can be achieved without error. It is only if some step in the process is omitted or improperly applied that the results turn out to be in error. The same is true here. Follow the procedure. Do it methodically, skipping nothing. Then you can have confidence in your results.

It is not simple, but it is straightforward.

## Do Not Abuse the Bible

The Bible is one of God's good gifts to us. It is his revelation. Far too often than most of us would care to admit, we have abused its message by failing to approach it properly. We have found a text that sounds good and used it without ever really knowing precisely what it said. Just as foolishly, we have skipped over texts through which God spoke a magnificent message just because we did not wish to make the effort to really understand them. Either approach is an abuse of God's word for which we shall be held accountable. Ezekiel was warned about his responsibility as a watchman over Israel (Ezek. 33:7-9). The same warning applies to us. We dare not fail to let God use the Bible to speak through us to his people.

Furthermore, it is an abuse of the Old Testament to expect it to say exactly what the New Testament says. If it did, there would have been no need for a New Testament. The early Christians certainly found riches in the Old Testament for preaching. It was the only Bible which they had. Jesus also found it filled with riches for him and for his followers. But it was not the end of the story. We must recognize that it always looked forward to the coming of God's Messiah. The New Testament is its fulfillment. We must see it as it is and not as we would like for it to have been. We must interpret the entire Bible, not just part of it.

## Let God Speak for Himself

In carrying the preceding thought just a bit further, we must remember that it is our task to let God speak through the Bible and through us to his people. We are responsible for bringing our best skills to the task of interpretation. But it must always be God who speaks. It is not our task to say what God could have said, or what we wish he had said, but rather to be channels of what he did say and is saying.

Furthermore, we must not be guilty of speaking with an uncertain sound. If we are not sure what God is saying through a particular passage, then we must lay it aside and move on to something else. Our lack of understanding of any one specific passage does not mean that God has no message there. Much more likely such a failure indicates either our ignorance of all the facts necessary or of our lack of skill in bringing what we do know to bear upon that passage. There is far too much of which we can be certain for us to carry our uncertainties to our audience.

I do not mean that we should not let those to whom we minister know that we are human. You should have no qualms in revealing to your class or congregation that there are passages which you do not understand. They do not expect you to have all knowledge. What I am suggesting is that it is unnecessary to try to present a message on a passage which you do not understand. Just put it aside and work on it longer.

Be sure that what you do teach or preach from the Bible is God's message. There are far too many places where you will hear his voice with clarity for you to spend your time in teaching or preaching on passages where his voice is only poorly heard.

God will speak through the pages of this ancient book if you will let him. Do not get in his way, but rather let his message flow through you to his people. It is a thrilling thing to know that God is using you to speak from his word to his people. Let God have all of your skills and all of your knowledge, and his message will flow. Remember, it is the biblical faith which says, "the word of our God will stand forever" (Isa. 40:8).

### Learn by Doing

There is no other way of learning how to interpret the Bible than to learn by doing. Reading this book and memorizing the necessary steps will be of no avail unless you actually gather the materials and begin the process. Now, it is not necessary at first to buy every book which I have suggested. Your church library, a public library, or a college or university library will be able to fill in the gaps. Books which they do not have can be ordered from other libraries.

But amassing all of the best reference books in the world still will not get the job done. It is as you begin to follow the process that you will discover how to do the job. Each time you sit down and try to interpret a passage, you will learn something which will make the next time easier. When you get tired, rest, but do not quit. You would never have learned to do anything worthwhile if you had quit whenever you stumbled, failed, or got tired. The same is true here. There is no substitute for doing it over and over again. Practice may not make you perfect, but it will make you a better, more confident interpreter.

I rejoice that you have been interested enough in the task of interpeting the Bible to read this book. I now encourage you to begin the task. Do not put it off for some other time. Start as soon as possible. I know that God's Spirit will bless you in the process. But far more important, in the process of interpreting God's Word, you will become a blessing to others. It is that to which he has called you.